WALKING

and TALKING

with GOD

Judy Pouilly

Createspace Publishing

First Edition

June 2017

Judy Pouilly
Hayward, WI 54843
judypouilly@gmail.com

ISBN #9781544218540

DEDICATION

To my lovely husband, Bob, who supported the family while I stayed home and listened to the Lord.

To my beautiful son, Marc, and my daughters, Robin and Mandy, who helped with editing and cover design.

And to my precious grandchildren, Jonathan, Joseph, Sara, Leah, Lucas and Matthew.

A special acknowledgement to Pastor Andrea Wittwer for getting this book out of the drawer and preparing it for publication.

May your God become a bigger God as you read these pages.

For everyone that uses milk is unskilled in the word of righteous: for he is a babe.
But strong meat belongeth to them that are full of age, even those who by reason of use have their senses trained to discern both good and evil.
Hebrews 5: 13-14 (KJV)

WALKING AND TALKING WITH GOD

CONTENTS

INTRODUCTION

Our walk with the Lord is like going up a stairway. Some people just stay on one step - not realizing the promises, joys and fulfillments they can know if they continue to walk with the Lord and grow in Him.

The beginning of this book is for those who are just starting their magnificent adventure of walking with the Lord. Moreover, it is also for those who had a first sweet experience with the Lord, but one that now seems far in the past. We all want to go beyond baptism and wonderful church activities to a real and personal relationship with our Lord. For such a walk is full of blessings and wisdom and bounty that far exceed what the world can give us.

Truly each chapter is wonderfully different and yet each chapter builds and matures beyond the preceding ones.

May all who are raising families and worrying about job security be blessed by these chapters and continue growing in their walk and talk with Jesus; a simple, close, strong walk of victory and blessings.

The latter part of this book is full of in-depth teachings that will bless people and help families stay together and overcome problems. Truly a simple, strong walk with the Lord is a great treasure and will enhance all that you do. Surely whether you don't know the Lord yet, or are a weary Christian; this book was written to encourage, uplift, teach, and refresh you.

And now may the Spirit of the Lord add to what you read and heap blessing upon blessing on you. And I will bless you, and so you shall be a blessing; and I will bless those who bless you (Genesis 12:2-3).

God told Abraham about this long ago when He said, "I will bless those in every nation who trust Me as you do. "And so, it is, that all who trust in Christ share the same blessing Abraham received." (Gal. 3:9 TLB)

1

VISIONS OF STAIRWAYS

Today brought another vision of stairways. How interesting and enjoyable it was, and a little bit different from the others. What a strange summer this has been. Truly the stairways were becoming the high point of my summer. They reminded me of the ladder in Jacob's dream.

> **Genesis 28:12-13 & 15-16** And he had a dream, and behold, a ladder was set on the earth with its top reaching up to heaven; and behold, the angels of God were ascending and descending on it. [13]And behold, the Lord stood above it and said, "I am the Lord, the God of your father Abraham and the God of Isaac; the land on which you lie, I will give it to you and your descendants. [15] "And behold, I am with you, and will keep you wherever you go, and will bring you back to this land; for I will not leave you until I have done what I have promised you. [16] Then Jacob awoke from his sleep and said, Surely the Lord is in this place and I did not know it."

I was just an ordinary housewife, raising two children. My husband had a difficult job and left it, expecting to get another one right away. This was quite a few years ago, when it was easier to change jobs.

Yet, as the days and weeks and even months started to go by, without a new job, we began to feel unsettled and fearful. I spent much of the time in the Bible. The Bible is amazingly helpful when we are in need and reading it would drive out the fear and unrest and leave peace, inner strength and trust.

The stairway visions came that summer. Some were the same ones, repeated, and others were different. One stairway was straight up - very steep. Fortunately, it was short, only about three steps and each step was white, as if lighted by light bulbs. Other stairways went up slowly and curved gently like peaceful mountain roads. Some stairways were slanted and looked exactly like stairways going from one floor to the next. All the steps were always light, but in some stairways, one step in the middle would be dark.

And finally, at the end of the summer when we were getting down to our last pennies, I saw this important vision. It was a normal stairway with the shape of two people standing at the top and looking down. I just knew that it meant victory and that my husband had a job and within two weeks he was working. Praise the Lord!

All the stairways seemed to denote growing in faith. The stairways with the one dark step came at the time when my husband would go on job interviews and not get hired. They were warnings ahead of time, not to trust in that interview.

How awesome that God would help me through that difficult summer with multiple visions, wonderful emotions, and foreknowledge of failed interviews and a future job.

My trust in God started to grow by leaps and bounds. My faith and belief, and the kind of Christian I was, grew that summer and has been growing ever since. Yes, God is stronger than the mightiest army and can open a way where there is no way. He is the God of the Bible. He so loves us and wants us to grow and mature in Him. It pleases Him whenever we turn to Him and trust Him to carry us until the time of victory.

Our walk with the Lord is very much like a stairway or ladder. We want to climb those steps and receive the blessings and rewards of the higher steps.

Hebrews 11:6 And without faith it is impossible to please him, for he who comes to God must believe that He is, and that He is a "rewarder" of those who seek Him.

Also, it is important that we don't skip the early steps. These are the foundation steps and they need to be as strong as the cement foundations of buildings.

Know ye not that ye are God's building; a royal priesthood, a holy nation, a people for God's own possession (I Corinthians 3:9 and I Peter 2:9).

Yes, firm foundation steps will always keep you and your ministries solid and secure. Thus, this book starts with the foundation steps, first, and then goes on to the higher steps.

2

TURNING TO THE LORD

Who turns to the Lord, but a person with an emptiness, problem, difficulty or need? And when we seek the Lord, as scripture says, we find Him.

Matthew 7:7 Ask, and it shall be given to you; seek, and you shall find; knock, and it shall be opened to you.

I was twenty-seven when I started seeking the Lord. I had reached all my goals in life and yet there was this emptiness inside - questioning about life.

Was this all?
Was there more?
What was I missing?

But, I couldn't understand why this feeling, of something missing, persisted; and I would remind myself that I was a registered nurse. For me, this was the most important career in the world, and I had even received a scholarship. Also, there was my super husband and two beautiful young children. I grew up in a vacationland area of Wisconsin and knew money wasn't the answer. People from the cities would come during the summer and rush around and not look peaceful or contented.

Oh, how wise is our Lord. He knew the kind of Christian witness that was just right for me. My family didn't attend church and I was full of unbelief. No one believes all that people say on television or in the newspapers and especially not in advertising. I didn't know if I should believe what people said when they quoted the Bible to me. I needed to see something, not just hear words. Anybody can say words and even embellish them.

Well, there I was driving my daughter to kindergarten when I met this mother who had peace. She was peaceful during spring cleaning and when her children had chicken pox and even if they ran short of money before pay day. This peace was what I needed, this was what I didn't have. But, where did she get it? The next time I saw her, she mentioned going to church on a week night. Instantly, like a light bulb turning on, I knew that it was from church and from God that this wonderful peace came - this peace that I so needed. I later learned about the Fruits of the Spirit in Galatians 5:22-23. What a witness these fruits are to hardhearted unbelievers who aren't affected by words but want to see something in Christians, that will start them seeking God.

Galatians 5:22-23 But the fruit of the Spirit is love, joy, peace, patience, kindness, goodness, faithfulness, gentleness, self-control; against such there is no law.

Again, I will say how important the Fruits of the Spirit are. For, surely, all people would want to know a joyful, loving, and peaceful person's God.

Life seems to produce a lot of needs. The need to be loved is chief among them. The fast pace of the business world produces a serious need to relax and unwind. Health, finances, and families create an additional wealth of needs.

Matthew 5:3 Blessed are the poor in spirit (needy), for theirs is the kingdom of heaven.

It is human nature to try and fulfill our needs ourselves. People have tried a multitude of things; even such things as material possessions, selfish desires, alcohol, drugs, activism, and so forth and yet they have failed to fulfill their own needs.

But the Almighty God, the Creator of Heaven and Earth, is faithful. He has the answers that mankind does not have in themselves. And His Love for us is healing to our souls and transforming to our lives. And so it is, thus, that even our needs become a blessing - because it is those very needs that turn us to the Lord. Therefore, let us be like Caleb and Joshua who turned fully to the Lord and did not die in the wilderness, like the rest of the men of the older generation, but they entered the Promised Land and were rewarded with special plots of land (Joshua 14:7-14 and 19:49-50).

Philippians 4:19 And my God shall supply all your needs according to His riches in glory in Christ Jesus!

3

BEGINNING YOUR WALK

My desire to go to church kept growing stronger and stronger. I knew the Lord had a beautiful peace to give us and whatever other good things He had to give us - I wanted those things, too.

As a child, my family didn't attend church and so I knew absolutely nothing about the Lord, the Bible or church. I was like a hungry person waiting to be filled and eager to make up for lost time. Therefore, I filled my time with reading the Bible from beginning to end, while I waited for my family to desire to come to church with me.

Then we moved and my thirtieth birthday occurred. Many of our new neighbors were young and they kidded me about being "over the hill." Well here I was, feeling old and not even baptized yet. I just couldn't wait any longer so I picked a church out of the phone book (one I thought my husband would approve of when he was ready to attend), and the children and I were in church the next Sunday.

How we enjoyed it and after a while my husband came, too. It was such a friendly church. But I seemed to know Jesus only as Savior and not yet as Lord - for I still had my temper. And I wanted more, I longed to be a new person like scripture says.

II Corinthians 5:17 Therefore if any man is in Christ,
He is a new creature; the old things passed away; behold,
new things have come.

A Lay Witness Weekend was coming to our church. My
husband and I helped the church to prepare for the weekend and
so we felt that we should attend. Our children were enjoying
sleeping in our partially finished basement, thus their bedrooms
were available and a wonderful couple spent that weekend with
us. How different these people seemed; God was so alive and
active in their lives - every day.

Certainly, Jesus suffered on the cross for us to live a more
victorious life. I deeply desired the Lord's peace and all the rest
of His blessings, that give us new life and makes us blessings to
those around us.

That weekend I really felt God's love for me. He knew me
better than I knew myself. He knew faults in me that I wasn't
even aware of and yet He loved me more than all my family,
friends, children, and parents put together. It was indescribable!
And it was glorious!

This tremendous love is so needed by our hearts, and it is
not found in the world or fame, but only in God. For surely, our
Creator must have created a place in each of us that stays empty
until He alone comes in and fills it.

Oh, how I needed to keep this love. So, I started going to
church all week long and I was becoming overly busy, just like
Martha, and yet I wasn't making any progress. It seemed like the
harder I tried the 'behinder' I got, until the Lord showed me the
teaching about Mary, the sister of Martha, in Luke 10:38-42.
Thereafter, one morning while I was sitting quietly at home,
reading the Bible, I heard God say in my heart:

"Do you want to please me?"

Everything was quiet and still as I listened and then He said, "Know me better."

Immediately, I asked God how to know Him better and His inner, still voice said, "The Bible and Prayer."

It was like an important thought, impressed upon my mind, and it brought peace, contentment, and a wonderful feeling.

The Bible is God's words, God's thoughts, God's dealings with people, and God Himself. And praying is just talking to God - simple words from our hearts and our needs.

Thus, a longing for righteousness, meaning, purpose, blessings, and help in life directs us to seek a personal relationship, or walk, with the Lord. The early steps of this walk will start to be revealed in Chapter Four and will continue throughout the rest of the book.

Matthew 5:6 Blessed (happy) are those who hunger and thirst for righteousness, for they shall be satisfied.

Reference - still small voice (I Kings 19:12 KJV).

4

FOUNDATION STEPS

BIBLE

So now, I knew that God wanted me to read the Bible. Through its pages, I would come to know Him better. For, how can we love what we don't know and how can we trust in God, before we come to know Him?

I bought an easier translation of the Bible to start with (The Living Bible), and our dear Lord provided the time. The children were off to school, my husband was off on a business trip and a snowstorm kept me at home. Therefore, I curled up with my Bible and a cup of coffee and I started at the beginning.

Now, I have always loved to read. The peace that came from this time was beyond describing. I know that no one could find this kind of peace in the world and even that millions of dollars couldn't buy it.

Thus, here I was trying to please God, by getting to know Him, and He was blessing me with an abundance of peace and happiness.

There are so many interesting things in the Bible. Do you know that Joshua (Chapter one, verse eight) says, if you read the Bible daily and do what it says, that you will prosper and succeed?

Joshua 1:8 This book of the law shall not depart from your mouth; but you shall meditate on it day and night, so that you may be careful to do according to all that is written in it; for then you will make your way prosperous, and then you will have success.

Also, Deuteronomy (Chapter twenty-eight) and Leviticus (Chapter twenty-six) are very similar chapters. They show us how to walk in blessings or curses. Both came upon the Old Testament people. When the people departed from obeying God's laws, commands, and teachings; they drifted away from God's blessings and into problems. Their problems eventually became so severe that they cried out to the Lord and started returning to Him, and then they could began walking all over again in blessings, health, peace in their country and prosperity.

The first Psalm tells us that the man who meditates on God's law, day and night, will be blessed, firmly planted, and will prosper at whatever he does. John 8:31-32 teaches us that if we abide in God's Word, then we are truly His disciples and will know the truth and will be set free. Surely, we all want to be free from striving, struggling, stumbling, and failing on our own. Luke 1:37 says, "For nothing shall be impossible with God."

Moreover, the gospels tell us that if His Word abides in us, we may ask whatever we will in prayer and it shall be answered. Thus, abiding in the Bible enables us to abide in the Lord and helps our prayers become much more effective (John 15:7).

Psalm 119:24 tells us that God's testimonies are our counselors and what an inexpensive and beautiful way to receive counsel. Praise the Lord! And so, how can one describe the Bible? I only know that when I'm in the Bible, I'm happier and healthier and life goes much more smoothly than ever before.

PRAYER

During the time when I first desired to grow in prayer, my right hand was covered by many small warts. It especially bothered me on Sunday mornings. I just couldn't get past those church greeters without shaking hands. So finally, I cried out to the Lord and told Him how awful my hand looked and how it was hard for me to shake hands and I asked for His help. The next Sunday came and I timidly stuck out my hand to shake it and it was totally free of warts - I mean all of them were gone! I knew God had done it. I deeply longed to learn how to talk to Him better - for there are a multitude of people who need answers to prayer. So, I read books on prayer and tried to follow what they said. I even wrote guide lines to adore, worship, confess, petition and intercede; and all that resulted in, was confusion.

Therefore, I decided to set some time apart for God every weekday morning. It was after the family was off to work and school and I was alone in the house. The time was very flexible. I tidied up a few things around the house and then came away to the Lord. I didn't pay attention to the clock and sometimes I started at nine and other times it varied, approximately a half hour either way. At times, I prayed for thirty minutes and many times, twice that long. The length of time depended on how many worries, concerns and needs I had that day.

When I first started learning how to pray, I asked the Father in Jesus' Name to teach me how to pray. I found myself telling God little things that made me anxious and asking the Lord to be in control of those things and work them out the way He thought was best. I poured out my worries to God and I couldn't believe how many I carried around, buried deep, down inside. I'm sure that other people carry many anxieties, fears and worries, too. As time went by I became more and more peaceful, joyful and contented.

I would worry when it snowed in the middle of the day. I had sent the children off on the school bus without boots, that morning, and the buses were old. What if they had a flat tire coming home and the kids had to stand out in the snow while it was fixed? Well, it was such a joy to give those "what ifs" to God and ask Him to be in control and work them out. I didn't have to worry the rest of the day and the bus never had a flat tire.

The last verse of Matthew says how the Lord will be with us, always.

Matthew 28:20b and lo, I am with you always, even to the end of the age.

I read a book called "The Practice of the Presence of God" by Brother Lawrence, during this time. I believed that God was in the room with me, hearing my prayers. I saw numerous small worries just fade away and vanish. If the Lord needed more time to work out the bigger problems, that was all right with me.

How wonderful not to carry those stressful worries around, even if they are small - just tell a powerful, loving, wise and Fatherly God about them.

At first, I would go into my bedroom and get on my knees and pray. But as time went on I would pray all through the house and especially where I sat comfortably with my Bible and cup of coffee. I would start by asking God to bless and heal the sick people I knew and open jobs for the unemployed people in my church and neighborhood and on and on. Sometimes, I imagine that Jesus is before me and I bow my head onto His lap and tell Him about everything and everyone I am concerned about. At times, I imagine the Lord on a throne and I kneel before Him and just soak up His peace, love and blessings. For surely the Lord created our imagination to be filled with Himself and not lesser things.

"Psalm 50:15 "Call upon Me in the day of trouble; I shall rescue you, and you will honor Me.""

It pleases our God when we ask His help. It is also a very wise thing to do. As Christians reach middle-age, many of them deepen their walk with the Lord. They do this by returning to the beginning where they first met Him. As they start their walk with God, all over again, it becomes a greater and much more powerful, anointed and blessed relationship. It is amazing what they get out of the Bible when they again start spending time in it like they did as new Christians. Moreover, their prayer life becomes sweet communion - sweet, sweet abiding in the Lord, for never has there been a Friend known to mankind who is so readily available, so everything that we need.

In conclusion, the Bible and Prayer are the greatest Foundation Steps for knowing the Lord, and they will always continue to be important even to the spiritually mature. The Bible is the Living Word and the more we grow, the more we learn from it. And likewise, growing in prayer and hearing from God makes our lives more blessed and abundant, more joyful and successful, and more of everything that is good.

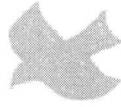

5

LORDSHIP AND THE HOLY SPIRIT

When I was thirty-two years old, I prayed and asked the Lord to take control of my life. I had controlled my life for thirty-two years and was not satisfied with where I was. Perhaps with the Lord in control of my life I would become more pleasing to myself and to God, more self-controlled, more temper free, more spiritual and more a blessing to others. One of the promises to Abraham, and all those who walk by faith, is to be blessed and become a blessing (Genesis - Chapter twelve).

If you have ever been around such people who are filled with the Lord's Presence - full of love and peace and joy and hope and positivity - you feel drawn to them like a magnet and know it is possible to grow closer to the Lord and become like them. They sit so calmly, filled with all those good feelings that overflow to people around them. Nowhere have I seen people drawn to a depressed person. Negative, hopeless and bitter feelings can fill and overflow to nearby people, too.

Matthew 6:33 But seek ye first His kingdom and His righteousness; and all these things shall be added to you.

15

I was becoming interested in the third person of the Trinity, the Holy Spirit. Perhaps the Holy Spirit could help me to become more of a blessing to my family and the people around me. I read many books about God's Spirit and became hungrier and hungrier. I also read about the gifts of the Holy Spirit, and that Satan may counterfeit them.

Well, I wanted to try tongues (speaking in other languages), but how did I know what was counterfeit and what was real? So again, I went to the Lord in prayer and told God that I didn't want to go to people for prayer for tongues but that I would really like Him to give it to me - alone and at home. Again, there was this uninterrupted time with the Lord as the children were in school and my husband was on another business trip.

How I enjoyed staying at home and reading and praying and even spending time praising the Lord. I was all prayed up, confessed up, interceded up, and I made sure that God knew I was all surrendered to Him (my heart, mind, even my words and etc.). Also, to be on the safe side, renounce having your fortune told in the past, and any other occult things as we are getting into the spiritual world of power, now.

Acts 1:8 but you shall receive power when the Holy Spirit has come upon you; and you shall be my witnesses both in Jerusalem, and in all Judea and Samaria, and even to the remotest part of the earth.

While praising the Lord, I spoke two syllables in another language. It didn't seem to be useful so I let it slide for a few months and then I tried it again. This time I spoke a paragraph that started with those same two syllables. Several different times when I was praying this way, I decided to give it up as I didn't know what I was saying. Each time I decided to stop, God told me what I was saying. I was saying, "Jesus Christ is Lord of Life," and I was singing the Doxology and parts from hymns.

I finally realized that the Lord didn't want me to give it up. I was praying and praising and talking to the Lord more perfectly in this language than I did in my own. Jesus seemed so close to me now, and so real, just as if He was walking alongside me and would help me with anything throughout the day. All I really needed to do was to remember to ask His help with the things I did during the day. I also knew that it was a good idea to thank the Lord after He had helped me, but I often forgot to do this. I didn't condemn myself for being forgetful, for there is much to learn and I was so pleased with how often I remembered to call on the Lord for help and at how successful those situations turned out.

John 14:16 And I will ask the Father, and He will give you another Helper (Paraclete, One called alongside, Comforter, Strengthener) that He may be with you forever. Also, see John 14:26

This experience lasted only about two weeks. Then I started to walk by faith, and like the promise in the last sentence of the Gospel of Matthew, I knew now by faith that the Lord was still with me. The Bible seemed more open to me, after this experience. The Cross became more meaningful and I knew that Jesus was my Savior two thousand years ago, and could still save me from anything I might get myself into, today. Perhaps I might say the wrong words over the telephone. If so, I could ask the Lord to forgive me, and erase those words (from their mind) and bless that person. I probably didn't say the wrong words but I am a worrier and I would rather ask Jesus' help than worry. Oh peace, peace, beautiful peace! A helper, a comforter is alongside and we don't know it unless we talk to Him. How safe, secure and loved I felt. I could have asked Him for help before I burned the cookies and I wouldn't have burned them. And on the way to church meetings, I could even ask the Lord to take my words out of my mind and keep it empty or fill it with His words.

Brother Lawrence, in his book "The Practice of The Presence of God" tells us how he asked for help with everything that he did throughout the day, even washing dishes. If it turned out satisfactorily he would thank the Lord, and if it didn't turn out okay he would ask the Lord what the Lord expected when he was left on his own.

And the promise of the Holy Spirit is for everyone who desires it. Just ask and seek for it.

> **Acts 2:38-39** And Peter said to them, "Repent, and let each of you be baptized in the name of Jesus Christ for the forgiveness of your sins: and you shall receive the gift of the Holy Spirit. [39] For the promise is for you and your children, and for all who are far off, as many as the Lord our God shall call to himself.

Seeking more of the Lord always benefits us, and all the steps in following Christ build and grow upon each other. Consequently, when we hunger to be more than just a busy Christian, but truly a new creation, we will desire that Christ be Lord of our lives and we will treasure the Comfort, Power, and Wisdom of His Holy Spirit.

God is the only one who can be Lord over our lives and yet set us free to be the best we can be. The Spiritual way seems truly mysterious and a paradox to our natural reasoning. For in the world when people lord it over others; they control, manipulate, command, and enslave. Yet our Lord gave His life for us, loves us, is for us (Psalm 118:6), serves us, and each day enables us to be wiser, better and more successful than we could be without Him.

Psalm 103: 1 Bless the Lord, O my soul; and all that is within me, bless His holy name.

Bless He who pardons, heals, redeems, crowns, satisfies and renews. Bless the Lord, O my soul.

6

THE PERFECTER

The first work of the Holy Spirit in my life seemed to be that of a Perfecter.

> **Hebrews 12:2a** "fixing our eyes on Jesus, the Author and Perfecter (finisher) of our faith,"

> **I Corinthians 3:16** "Do you not know that you are a temple of God, and that the Spirit of God dwells in you?"

First, the Lord removed idols from my life, and placed Himself in His rightful place of Lordship. All other things that are in first place in our lives are idols and can be "shaken" (Hebrews 12:26-28). Only Jesus is a firm foundation. The Bible also tells us that Jesus is the sole name in which people can be saved.

> **Acts 4:12** And there is salvation in no one else; for there is no other name under heaven that has been given among men, by which we must be saved.

Self is often the number one idol. Self is never satisfied and it always covets more. Only in God's way, will we find happiness, purpose and meaning. We know that to be a movie star or a wealthy businessman or a retired person does not bring inner peace and contentment. This is much more fully found, in our Creator's wiser will for us.

Another big idol is our husbands and in reverse situations, wives. It is right to submit and obey your husbands, but don't put them in the place of God in your heart. Allow spouses to be human and have weak areas. Only God is perfect and unchangeable.

When both the husband and wife seek God's will there will be harmony and no need to compromise. The Lord is big enough to change either mate's will to allow the other to obey Him. If a spouse opposes their mate's serving the Lord - then perhaps God is allowing it as a training time or a waiting time upon the Lord. Waiting times are special times to fill up with the Bible, grow in prayer, raise our families and mature in Christ.

Children can become idols. How we love them and yet God has given them to us for a time, and loves them even more then we do. Seeing God's great love for them makes it easier for us to let them grow up and move away, as adults.

A big, beautiful house can become an idol. My yard used to be an idol to me. I kept it completely free of weeds and was so proud of it. Then the Lord spoke to my heart and said that the people on my street were far more important than my grass. They had souls that could be lost or saved and my grass didn't. So, my priorities were rearranged and I spent less time in the yard. I have some weeds now, and when I don't have time to water, it often rains. Praise the Lord!

A job can become an idol and mean more to us than the Lord. A job is also an untrustworthy foundation, as it can lay people off. But how wonderful it is that our Lord is always with us. He never deserts us, even though we often do likewise to Him. Yes, He is near us all the time - we need only talk to Him to be aware of His Comforting Presence.

What is in the Lord's place (first place in our hearts and minds) is often what we trust in. A bank savings is more visible than the Lord, but an illness could wipe it out. Thankfully, the Bible tells us that God remains the same, yesterday, today and forever.

Our churches, denominations and pastors deserve our respect and love. But our worship, trust and number one place in our hearts and thoughts belong to the loving, faithful, unchangeable and forgiving Lord who went to the cross for us.

All these important things need Jesus over them. The world needs Jesus. He is the Way, and the Truth, and the Life, and may we point needy people to Him.

John 14:5-6 Thomas said to Him, "Lord, we do not know where You are going, how do we know the way?" ⁶ Jesus said to him, I am the Way, and the Truth, and the Life; no one comes to the Father, but through Me.

I needed this wise, loving Lord in all areas of my life and I was quick to invite Him into the needy areas. After a minor traffic accident, I was nervous about driving and each time I entered the car, I asked the Lord to come with me and give me a safe trip - which He did.

But, baking cakes from scratch was something I had done since I was a child. It was so natural that I would forget to ask the Lord into this part of my life. The Lord's sense of humor taught me to remember Him in this area, too. Several angel food cakes in a row had strange and comical problems. They would fall apart, or the shape would be so unusual that I couldn't help but laugh, and so forth. I hurried to the grocery store and bought cookies for my company and gave the strange looking cakes to my children. It tasted great and they enjoyed the situation. For a while after that, I made angel food cakes with trepidation and remembered to ask the Lord's help and blessings. All succeeding cakes have turned out fine.

Another beautiful area where the Lord showed me His Lordship was when the children became ill. I was a nurse and nurses rush straight to doctors when someone is ill. Well, my husband had a summer of unemployment and doctor's office visits seemed kind of costly. So, that year I learned to pray first, before I took them to a doctor. Many times, they would improve dramatically during the night and be healthy the next morning, after praying. I remember my daughter having chest congestion and pain and my son having a sprained and swollen ankle. Those evenings I prayed and was all set to go to the doctor the next day. But the next day, the chest pain was gone and the congestion was being coughed up, and my son could walk on his ankle without any pain.

It was not my prayers but the One who answers prayer. I would gently touch the area needing healing and ask the Lord Jesus to touch it, and then thank Him and be prepared to go to the doctor the next day if it was necessary. For our God, can work through doctors also and bless both them and us.

My son's friend hurt his finger in school sports. We gently touched it and asked the Lord Jesus to touch and heal it; we gave thanks, and then he went to the doctor. Sure enough, it was broken and he was supposed to wear a splint but he never did and in a few days, it was fine.

Children have such a simple and marvelous trust, and are much easier to pray for than logical adults. Mankind can make prayer so hard and confusing and complicated, while God simplifies it. God is the helper, the One who answers prayer. His job is the greater job. We just, simply ask our Heavenly Father's help. And the understanding of prayer and the timing of the answers, we leave up to the Lord.

Revelation 22:13 "I am the Alpha and the Omega, the first and the last, the beginning and the end".

Yes, Jesus who came from God and shows us what God is

23

like, is worthy to be our Lord. He was, and is, and is to come. Praise the Lord.

> **Isaiah 53:4-5** Surely our griefs He Himself bore, and our sorrows He carried; Yet we ourselves esteemed Him stricken, smitten of God, and afflicted. ⁵ But He was pierced through for our transgressions, He was crushed for our iniquities; the chastening for our well-being fell upon Him, and by His scourging (stripes, wounds) we are healed.

These lovely verses show us what the Lord did for us on the Cross. It seems strange for us to believe that someone could love us enough to die for us. Truly this love is beyond human comprehension.

The Psalms also tell us about the Lord being a refuge, a shelter, a deliverer, and on and on. Yet, God has created everyone with a free will and he honors that free will. If we want Him to be Lord of our life - we must ask Him in, think of Him and talk to Him during the day, and seek His right way of living.

But sadly enough, we can drift away from Him at any time and struggle through life on our own. When this happens, and it often does without our realizing it; we need only turn back to Him to find our true Friend, our Lord and His abundant forgiveness, counsel and blessings. Amen.

7

RENEWING THE MIND

Jesus comes into our lives and minds to renew them. Our goal as Christians is to become more like Him.

Romans 8:29 For whom he foreknew, he also predestined to become conformed to the image of his Son, that he might be the first-born among many brethren;

Yes, we are to become more and more like Christ and more and more a blessing to those around us and more ready for heaven.

Romans 12:1 tells us to be a living sacrifice. In other words, to live to please the Lord and not ourselves or friends; for by pleasing the Lord we will really be a true blessing to ourselves and others. Romans 12:2 says that when our minds are renewed we will know God's perfect will.

Romans 12:1-2 I urge you therefore, brethren, by the mercies of God, to present your bodies a living and holy sacrifice, acceptable to God, which is your Spiritual service of worship. ² And do not be conformed to this world, but be transformed by the renewing of your mind, that you may prove what the will of God is, that which is good and acceptable and perfect.

Jesus and His Precious Holy Spirit are busy restoring and refreshing us on the inside. And as Paul says, we are truly becoming temples of the Spirit of God.

But what is wanted of us? What is our new nature to be like? The Lord wants us to bear the fruits of His Holy Spirit and the verses on the fruits of the Spirit are a beautiful definition of a renewed personality.

Galatians 5:22-23 But the fruit of the Spirit is love, joy, peace, patience, kindness, goodness, faithfulness, gentleness, self-control; against such there is no law.

The verses just before Galatians 5:22 are descriptions of the old, unrenewed nature. I will include these verses only so that we can compare the difference and see what our old natures are capable of and realize how great is the need for renewal.

Galatians 5:19-21a Now the deeds of the flesh are evident, which are: immorality, impurity, sensuality, [20]idolatry, sorcery, enmities, strife, jealousy, outbursts of anger, disputes, dissensions, factions, [21a] envying, drunkenness, carousing, and things like these-

What dreadful verses these are. Truly a whole book could be written on renewal of the mind. How fortunate we are that forgiveness and help are readily available.

*   *   *

One of the first things the Lord taught me was to get enough sleep. Our bodies are human and need sleep and it is very, very difficult for us to be pleasant when we are overtired.

So, with my permission, the Lord started working on my attitudes. What a big and long lasting job that has turned out to be. It is very easy to see how anger can trap a person into acting and speaking foolishly and our God longs to set us free and help us act wisely and victoriously.

Ephesians 4:26-27 If you are angry, don't sin by nursing your grudge. Don't let the sun go down with you still angry - get over it quickly; [27]for when you are angry you give a mighty foothold to the devil. (TLB)

Frequently, the Lord will use us as a peacemaker or an encourager and how wonderful and exciting that is. For God blesses the peacemaker along with those holding opposing points of view. Only the Lord can diffuse difficult situations by giving us (His peacemakers) balanced and wise words to speak, and then His peace reigns and the one who spoke Godly words is blessed with indescribable joy.

Matthew 5:9 Blessed are the peacemakers, for they shall be called sons of God.

It is most often in difficult situations that negative and unhealthy attitudes pop up in us. The first attitude that the Lord and I tackled was self-pity. Many hours can be wasted by self-pity, and oh, how it keeps self on the throne and your mind filled with self. I could not stay in self-pity and keep the Lord in control of my life or keep my mind filled with Him. So, I resolved to give it up and even confessed it as wrong, and then I asked the Lord to help me put my mind back on Him.

Self-will is similar and even destroyed Judas. It seemed to

make him greedy and unwise. Self-will and thirty pieces of silver, for betraying Jesus, only brought a sad end to the life of Judas. The God who went to the cross for us, in the form of Jesus, has far more wisdom and a better plan for our lives, than we do.

> **Jeremiah 29:11-14a** 'For I know the plans that I have for you', declares the Lord, 'plans for welfare and not for calamity to give you a future and a hope. [12] Then you will call upon Me and come and pray to Me, and I will listen to you. [13] And you will seek Me and find Me, when you search for Me with all your heart. [14a] 'And I will be found by you,' declares the Lord, 'and I will restore your fortunes and will gather you-

Depression is a serious and important thing to work on. Depression is simply getting one's mind off the Lord. Consequently, people's minds are filled with doubt and then they progress to fear and then finally to depression. Such people are not looking to God and not trusting Him and they are full of unbelief and hopelessness. Depression is widespread today. There are many levels of depression and everybody works to overcome depression at one time or another in their lives.

Oh, how we must train our eyes and minds to return to the Lord and keep them there. When our mind is on a problem, the problem becomes bigger and bigger until that is all we see. God becomes smaller and farther away. If we take our minds off the problem and call on God - God becomes greater and our trust grows in the Lord's ability to handle the problem. Peace returns and the problem shrinks. What we focus on becomes bigger. If we focus on God, He becomes bigger and we can trust Him. Likewise, if we focus on the problem, it mushrooms and we sink into despair.

We read in the Bible and see how the people of the Bible

waited and trusted in God. Some people waited years before God gave them a son. Such people were Abraham and Sarah, Isaac and Rebekah, Rachel, and Hannah.

Genesis 16:1a Now Sarah, Abraham's wife, had borne him no children.

Genesis 18:10-14 Then the Lord said, "I will surely return to you about this time next year, and Sarah your wife shall have a son." Now Sarah was listening at the entrance to the tent, which was behind him. [11] Abraham and Sarah were already old and well advanced in years, and Sarah was past the age of childbearing. [12]So Sarah laughed to herself as she thought, "After I am worn out and my master is old, will I now have this pleasure?" [13] Then the Lord said to Abraham, "Why did Sarah say, 'Will I really have a child now that I am old?' [14] Is anything too hard for the Lord? I will return to you at the appointed time next year and Sarah will have a son." (NIV)

I always turn to prayer and the Bible to resist depression, asking the Lord's help and then filling up with His Words. Some people find it helpful to fill their homes with praise and worship music.

Jealousy and covetousness are awful attitudes. Jealousy so consumed and controlled King Saul that he tried to kill David. Saul was disobedient to God and full of torment. No one wants that. Being in the center of God's will, brings inner peace. A person who fears emotional problems needs to draw much closer into the safety, protection and peace of God's will.

Micah 6:8b And what does the Lord require of you but to do justice, to love kindness, and to walk humbly with your God.

Impatience, resentment, bitterness, unforgiveness and un-thankfulness, all need the Lord's help. The Apostle Paul tells us that it is God's will for us to give thanks.

I Thessalonians 5:18 in everything give thanks, for this is God's will for you in Christ Jesus.

Bitterness and resentment can become worse and worse as a person grows older if they don't admit them to the Lord and ask His help. Forgiving others helps us to be healthier, frees us inside, and allows us to receive blessings from God.

Matthew 6:12, 14-15 And forgive us our debts, as we also have forgiven our debtors. [14] For if you forgive men for their transgressions, your heavenly Father will also forgive you. [15] But if you do not forgive men, then your Father will not forgive your transgressions.

If an offense appears too big for us to forgive on our own, we need only ask the Lord's help. It pleases Him when we ask His help and we may do so over and over.

Worry, doubt, fear, anxiety and impatience are felt by all of us. They also show that at these moments we aren't trusting and focusing on the Lord. It is time to start turning to God, asking His help, and reading the Bible. God's Word increases our faith and it says that we have not because we ask not (and we especially need to ask for wisdom).

James 1:5 But if any of you lacks wisdom, let him ask of God, who gives to all men generously and without reproach, and it will be given to him.

The Bible teaches us to never avenge ourselves - that is the Lord's job. The Bible also says that we are to love and pray "good" for our enemies if we want to be God's children.

Matthew 5:44-45 But I say to you, love your enemies and pray for those who persecute you [45] in order that you may be sons of your Father who is in heaven; for He causes the sun to rise on the evil and the good, and sends rain on the righteous and the unrighteous.

Some people may be hard for us to love but we can start by praying blessings on them. This is when we are most made in the image of God, for these people praying blessings become creative and their minds grow free and healthy and blessed.

The Lord and I have had to do a lot of work on criticizing and judging. Satan is the accuser of the brethren and I sure don't want to assist him. Yet it seems like my mind is naturally critical when left on its own. As I'm becoming more aware of this tendency, I confess it and ask the Lord's help just as often as I need to.

However, when the Lord shows you a problem in someone and it is discernment, you are to pray and intercede for that person in private, and that is not judging but a part of intercession. In fact, whenever we catch ourselves judging someone, let us turn it into a blessing-prayer and share with God in His creativeness. Now blessing-prayers are simply praying opposite the problem, so if someone is mean we pray the Lord's love and kindness on them and so on.

People are sort of like transmitters. If we are filled with depression, it will transmit to those nearby us. If we have bitterness within, it will eventually come out in sharp words and can't be hidden. We must go to God for help. If we are filled with joy and love and peace and faith in God, it also isn't hidden and overflows to those around us. Being a Godly transmitter has an added blessing of being beneficial to our own health. Moreover, our world is truly in need of Godly transmitters.

THE REMEDY

When I have one of the above-mentioned attitudes, I first confess it to God as wrong. Then I say that I'm putting it under Christ's Lordship and I ask Him, by His power, to clean it out of me. At first, it was often that I needed to confess an attitude to the Lord and ask His power and help to overcome it.

The Spirit has a huge job in renewing the inside of us. But how we all need it, and how wonderful that God loves us and longs to do it. As time goes by and we see some progress and victory and freedom, we like ourselves more and thank God for what He is doing, what only the Lord can do as we allow Him to.

Our goal is to become more like Christ (Romans 8:29), and our new character has the fruits of the Spirit (Galatians 5:22-23) in it. Oh, the wonderful emotions, terrific feelings, blessings, and success as we grow up in the Lord.

- A **Baby Christian** is weak, helpless, lacking in understanding, and needs to be taken care of.
- A **Child Christian** is stubborn, wants their own way, and demands attention. Their emotions are not under control and they can cause strife.
- A **Young Adult Christian** is submissive to God's will and supportive of leaders. These people are strong in the Bible and prayer and can overcome adversity. They are moving upward and onward.
- A **Parental (Fatherly-Motherly) Christian** is full of love.

These people trust God and rest in Him - even in times of tribulation. They rejoice in today and look forward to what the Lord will bring on the next day. They see God in all situations.

32

They are strong and wise and yet gentle – and all people want to be around them.

8

LEAH

The story of Leah starts in the Twenty-Ninth Chapter of Genesis. The names of Leah's children are very important. They show us spiritual growth, a turning point and eventually victory in her life.

Leah was married to Jacob. Her sister Rachel was also married to Jacob and it was Rachel that Jacob loved. He was tricked by his father-in-law into marrying Leah. Now these two sisters had two problems to overcome. Leah wanted to be loved and Rachel was barren and wanted children.

The name of Leah's first child was Reuben. His name means **The Lord Has Seen** my misery (NIV, Chapter Thirty). She hoped that this child would make her husband love her. Her second child was named Simeon. Simeon's name means **The Lord Has Heard** that I am not loved and so He has blessed me with another son.

When she conceived, and gave birth to a third son, Leah named him Levi. Levi means **Attached** and she expected this from her husband because she had borne him three sons. Out of the twelve tribes of Israel, Levi was the tribe chosen to be the priestly tribe. They were attached to God.

When Leah gave birth to her fourth son, she gave praise to the Lord and named him Judah. Judah means **Praise**. Jesus, the Savior of the world, came from the tribe of Judah. Judah also led the tribes in the wilderness with Moses.

Numbers 10:14 The divisions of the camp of Judah went first, under their standard. Nahshon son of Amminadab was in command. (NIV)

Leah stopped having children, for a time, and Rachel was very jealous and demanded that Jacob give her children through her maidservant Bilhah. Then Bilhah gave birth to Dan, which means "He has vindicated" and also to Naphtali, which means "my struggle". Whereupon, Leah did what her sister did and gave her maidservant, Zilpah to Jacob. Zilpah gave birth to Gad, and Gad's name means **What Good Fortune**. Leah's maid also gave birth to Asher and Asher means **Happy.**

So, we see that as Leah stopped complaining and started praising God, she felt fortunate and happy. A thankful attitude became a powerful turning point in Leah's life. She still may not have had her husband's love but she had love from the Lord and from many sons.

Next, Leah was blessed with another son and his name was Issachar. Issachar means God has **Rewarded** me. Moreover, Leah again conceived and bore her final son. His name was Zebulun and Zebulun means **Honor**.

Having sons was very important to the Hebrew people. The choosing of their names and the meanings of those names were of great significance. The names that Leah picked give us a good deal of insight into her life. It is pleasing to note the progression of spiritual growth and maturity in her life as revealed by her son's names, in order of their birth.

Reuben	GOD HAS SEEN
Simeon	GOD HAS HEARD
Levi	ATTACHED
Judah	PRAISE
Gad	WHAT GOOD FORTUNE (by Leah's maid)
Asher	HAPPY (by Leah's maid)
Issachar	REWARDED
Zebulun	HONOR

I suppose that Jacob still may have loved Rachel. But as Leah turned from complaining to praise, she felt fortunate, happy, rewarded and honored. What a wonderful woman to be around. I would much rather live with Leah than a jealous, demanding Rachel.

Finally, God remembered Rachel and gave her a son named Joseph. Joseph means "May He add to me another son." At this time, Jacob returned with all his family and all his flocks to the Promised Land. Rachel stole her father's household idols and brought them with her into the Promised Land. A short time after entering the land of God's promises, Rachel died giving birth to her second son, Benjamin.

Perhaps her early death was related to the stealing and bringing of idols into the Promised Land, and the trouble it almost caused between her husband and father, and the curse her husband gave when innocently accused of stealing (Genesis 31:32)? This I don't know, however like all the rest of us imperfect people, Rachel belonged to God and history speaks well of her.

God additionally blessed Leah with the only daughter in the family and her name was Dinah. Leah now became the mother of the whole family. She was also the only wife that was buried with Jacob, in the same tomb as Abraham and Sarah, and Isaac and Rebekah.

As Leah laid aside the old-nature with its jealousy, strife, resentments, and relationship problems, she grew into her new, godly nature.

> **II Corinthians 2:15** As far as God is concerned there is a sweet, wholesome fragrance (perfume) in our lives. It is the fragrance of Christ within us, an aroma to both the saved and the unsaved all around us. (TLB)

Yes, as Leah started praising, she became a victorious overcomer and was honored by God.

Leah overcame her problem and perhaps her story can help other people. Numerous people have financial problems, health problems, emotional problems, stress problems and problems raising children. So, if we are lacking in hair, sort of short, plump, timid, in poor health and on and on; we can turn to the Lord and with His help our attitudes can change into those that lead to victory. May praise so change you that you become on "top of life" and "beautiful" from the inside out.

We must realize that this change that Leah went through did not happen overnight, that it was a process - yea even a walk with God.

I know that good can come out of problems and I know that problems have been around all throughout history. The Bible heroes were people just like us and their problems brought out a greatness and a power in them. Thus, Leah shows us that the first step in overcoming problems is to turn to the Lord. Also, she shows us an important and mysterious key to victory and that is changing from complaining to praise. The following chapters will go into greater detail about how to react to difficulties in ways that are Godly, right, creative and victorious. We want to learn how to react in the new spiritual way that attracts blessings, instead of repeating the old nature's frustrations and defeats.

I pray that the problems in your life will turn you to the Lord and that the Lord will redeem those problems and transform you into a special person. Amen - may it be so.

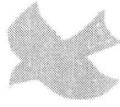

9

PRAISE

Philippians 3:1 Finally, my brethren, rejoice in the Lord. To write the same things again is no trouble to me, and it is a safeguard for you.

Praise is very powerful and very important. It renews the mind, it changes our attitudes from focusing on ourselves (which leads to self-pity) to focusing on the Lord, it makes us a blessing to those around us; and of even more importance an attitude of praise helps us to receive blessings from God. Even doctors say that patients with positive attitudes have a much greater chance of overcoming diseases and getting healed. Also, praising the Lord is an effective way to resist depression. Whether the time is short or long, praise is a major part of the path out of problems and into victory. Praise shows belief in God and can even hasten the victory.

King Jehoshaphat, in the Old Testament, used praise when faced with three huge enemy armies at the same time. His country was small and his people were scared and they had nowhere else to turn but to the Lord. Moreover, the Lord was not only trustworthy but He rewarded those who trusted in Him with the goods, garments, and valuable things of the enemy armies.

II Chronicles 20:20-22 Early the next morning the army of Judah went out into the wilderness of Tekoa. On the way, Jehoshaphat stopped and called them to attention. "Listen to me, O people of Judah and Jerusalem," he said. "believe in the Lord your God, and you shall have success! Believe his prophets, and everything will be all right!" [21] After consultation with the leaders of the people, he determined that there should be a choir leading the march, clothed in sanctified garments and singing the song "His Lovingkindness Is Forever" as they walked along praising and thanking the Lord! [22] And at the moment they began to sing and to praise, the Lord caused the armies of Ammon, Moab, and Mount Seir to begin fighting among themselves, and they destroyed each other! (TLB)

It is not just praise, but it is the Lord whom we praise - it is He who is all things to us. Often, we learn to praise God (or in simpler words – just give thanks) in the difficult times. In the book of Psalms, we see that David grew in praise during the time that King Saul was chasing him with all his armies. He was jealous of David and wanted to put him to death (because David was a better soldier and had God's anointing), even though David had not done anything wrong.

Frequently in the Psalms, David tells his soul not to be cast down, for he would yet praise the Lord.

Psalms 43:5 Why are you in despair, O my soul? And why are you disturbed within me? Hope in God, for I shall again praise Him, the help of my countenance, and my God.

Some mornings I may get out of bed feeling sort of down.

There doesn't seem to be any reason for it except that possibly the day is overcast and cloudy. If I can't shake off this heaviness, I will go get my prayer notebook and write down what I should be thankful for. I start with a free country, libraries (because I love to read), food, shelter, answered prayers, and so forth and before I know it the whole page is filled. As I go farther and farther back, I see lots and lots of prayers that have been answered and I start to feel much better.

Nehemiah 8:10b for the joy of the Lord is your strength.

At the beginning of this book, I mentioned that I started growing in the Lord the summer my husband was unemployed. I believe that God helps all His children through these difficult times. But those people who turn to Him in trust and stop complaining, are blessed with a tremendous peace and perhaps visions and a multitude of other blessings, and then in return they become blessings.

Genesis 12:2-3a "And I will make you a great nation, and I will bless you, and I will make your name great; and so, you shall be a blessing, [3a] and I will bless those who bless you, and the one who curses you I will curse.

The giving of thanks is a Biblical command that protects us. It helps keep our minds righteous before the Lord and helps us to keep out resentments. David gave thanks to the Lord continually in the book of Psalms. I don't believe that it is possible to renew our minds, mature in the Lord, or become victorious without learning to give thanks and praise to the Lord.

If I was one of those people with Moses in the wilderness, I would want to be one that was thankful for the manna, protection, clothes not wearing out and shoes not decaying; instead of one of the murmurers who made God angry.

Nehemiah 9:21 For forty years you sustained them in the wilderness; they lacked nothing, their clothes did not wear out nor did their feet become swollen. (NIV) See also Deuteronomy 29:5.

That is exactly what happened to me. After the summer of unemployment and all our savings had run out, my husband received a lower paying job. During this time, I had some inexpensive clothing that never wore out. I wore those same clothes day after day and year after year. I also didn't feel that I could easily afford going to the dentist. I took my children each year, but for five years, I stayed away and carefully brushed and flossed my own teeth. My teeth were perfect during this time. Several years later, when I had a job and our first dental insurance, I depended on this terrific insurance and developed an abscessed tooth. I have also stated earlier about praying for our children when they were ill and seeing them become better. I don't understand this, and we can now afford doctors and dentists; but one thing I know - call on the Lord and trust in Him - for there are some needs that only the Lord can meet.

God is the same, yesterday, today and forever. Just like He was with Moses in the wilderness, He will also be with us and take care of us in our wilderness times.

Whether the Lord stretched our money or whatever, we always paid all our bills and we have an excellent credit rating. We learned to be wise stewards of what we had. Often, we did without vacations, to save money, and I cut and permed our hair. My husband fixed our cars and appliances and so forth. We economized, attended church, tithed, took care of our family, spent time in the Bible and prayer, and gave thanks.

Psalms 50:23 "He who offers a sacrifice of thanksgiving honors Me; and to Him who orders his way aright I shall show the salvation of God."

Sometimes when I'm praying for everyone that God brings to my mind and my prayer list grows long, I just praise the prayer list. In other words, I thank God for each person and how He will help them and redeem each situation. I know that God will carry each person (if they allow Him to) until the problems pass and victory comes. Moreover, I know that the Lord can also help each person become stronger and wiser from these ordeals.

As we focus our minds on God and give thanks (praise), problems just seem to become smaller and simpler. And we can ask for and receive a wisdom and grace from the Lord that is supernatural.

Truly life sometimes seems incomprehensible. Yet, what seems to us as insurmountable can be full of possibilities for our God. He can create miracles, increase our faith, give us new teachings, give us love, reveal Himself to us, give us a testimony, blessings, and on and on. Then when everything turns out beautifully and we know that it wasn't our doing but help from the Lord, we can give thanks again and even that blesses us.

Recently, I went to a doctor and found out that my blood pressure was high. A couple weeks later I had some mild chest pain and was admitted to a hospital. All the heart tests turned out okay and how I praised the Lord! Finally, when the doctor was satisfied with my blood pressure and the medicine for it, he told me that my mammogram was questionable. I had hoped to quit seeing doctors for a while and here I had to go back for an ultrasound. With the weekend, in there, it was a long wait for the x-ray results to be mailed to my doctor.

During the wait, the Lord gave me the following teaching from the Bible. It is about Paul and takes place in the last couple chapters of the book of Acts.

Paul was a prisoner and on his way to Rome when he was

43

shipwrecked. Paul gave thanks on the ship during a lengthy storm and just before the ship was wrecked. Next, he was washed up on the island of Malta and bitten by a poisonous snake. He just seemed to keep giving thanks, exactly like the last half dozen or so chapters in the book of Psalms.

Secondly, God told me that Paul was kept safe in everything. He wasn't harmed as a prisoner, or in the shipwreck, or from the snake venom. Praise the Lord!

And yes, my ultrasound came back with a good report.

Thirdly, great ministry resulted from Paul's trip - a trip most people would label a "bummer of a trip." Paul encouraged everyone on the ship and prayed for all their lives to be saved. What a testimony. Next, when the poison from the snake didn't harm Paul, the islanders brought all their sick people to him and he prayed for them and everyone was healed.

Truly a lot more could be written about praise. The whole Bible is full of praise, and we are to praise because it is beneficial to us. Moreover, if we want another example of praise and the blessings that follow, we can read about Paul in jail in (Acts Chapter 16) and the earthquake and salvations that follow.

God's love and gentleness and kindness for us are unconditional. It is even there when we have faults, and it is this special love that woos us closer to Him. We need to give unconditional love and kindness to our families and others just like God does to us. Yes, we need to become loving and supportive and forgiving and pray creative blessings on the weak areas in others.

What a great trade-in we have with the Lord. We give Him our love and receive His greater love back. We give Him our worries and problems and receive His peace, wisdom, and powerful help. We give Him our sins and receive His grace, forgiveness and strength to lead a new life. We give Him a little of our time and receive more of His time and on and on.

"Prison to Praise" is a good book on the subject of praise by Merlyn Carothers.

I have seen a vision of people who were praising God. They were walking on top a range of mountains and holding onto Jesus' hands. Even in the midst of difficulties - the difficulties were beneath their feet and they were walking on top of them with the Lord. And in time those problems passed away as the mountain range became a flat plateau, with the Lord and the people standing on top. Praise the Lord!

Through every life some problems fall. May any that come into your life draw you closer to the Lord and to praise, and protect you from becoming negative and hurting. For the Bible says that God inhabits the praises of His people.

Psalm 22:3 But thou art holy, O thou that inhabitest the praises of Israel. (KJV)

And let everything that has breath, praise the Lord for He alone is worthy!

10

RAISING REWARDING TEENS

The teenage years frequently remind me of Christians growing Spiritually in the Lord. Sometimes teenagers act and sound grown-up and wise and at other times they will act childlike and immature. These are serious years and they are full of constant change and creativity.

> **Luke 1:80** And the child grew and became strong in spirit; and He lived in the desert until he appeared publicly to Israel. (NIV)

> **Luke 2:52** And Jesus grew in wisdom and stature, and in favor with God and men. (NIV)

This is also a beautiful time for parents to grow in their prayer lives and become prayer warriors. For this is what our Lord is doing now, having already finished His work on the cross and His great teachings, He has become our primary prayer partner and counselor; and likewise, we become the same for our growing children.

Teenagers are busy developing their own identities and goals in life and it is a time when parents need to be positive and encouraging. Encouragement is a gift of the Holy Spirit that is greatly needed today.

When our children were first starting school, I praised and encouraged them in a few things and it seemed to grow into more and more things to praise and encourage them in. Consequently, they always seemed to be good students.

I have known parents who were genuinely worried about their children's grades and they meant well, yet they were completely unaware of how critical their words were becoming. Our God created the stars and universe with His words and even though we don't understand it, our words also create after their kind - encouraging words to more success and negative words to more failure
.

I remember when our son had broken a bone bicycling and another one roller skating. When he went out to play I caught myself saying, "Now be careful, don't go so fast and don't break another bone." Those were the wrong kind of words to plant in his mind. I had to quit mentioning broken bones and plant good and creative words in his mind while I silently prayed for his safety. The years have passed and he has taken up skiing and other sports and thankfully no more bones have been broken.

What a wonderful and important job it is to be a parent. Our children have been a joy and a delight to us. Those very words came home on one of their kindergarten report cards and they have proven to be true over the years.

Truly every child is unique. Never label a child as lazy (or even worse), but quickly replace those words with better ones. Always hunt for and focus on the positive points in each child's personality. For the strong willed may be natural leaders and organizers, the mellow may have great spiritual potential, and the energetic may be strong in the gift of serving. Surely our Lord is a marvelous Creator and everyone is a little different from everyone else. Moreover, when the different personalities are under God's control, these people can become as special as our Bible heroes.

Meanwhile our children grew in confidence and went on to graduate in the third and fourth position of their high school classes. Then they were ready for college and I encouraged them to major in the subject they found easiest to get an A in, because I believed they had a natural talent in that area and would want to spend the rest of their lives in an area that came naturally to them and one they wouldn't have to struggle in.

Peer pressure is a very real and strong force for teenagers. We allowed our children to pick out the church we attended during their teen years. It is easy for parents to attend Bible studies, Women's Aglow meetings, Full Gospel Businessmen's meetings and etc. at any time. Our children chose a large church with an active youth group. Between school activities, study time, advanced classes and church activities, they did not have time to become bored or get into trouble.

Our oldest child is very intelligent, an over-achiever, and probably could be called strong-willed. The Junior High years seemed to have the most peer pressure. A strong child wants to make their own decisions and yet they are hesitant. I repeatedly told her how I loved her and how I wanted what was best for her and how I wanted the neighbors and everyone to love her. When she was invited to parties, we allowed this determined child to help make the decision whether to attend or not. I told her if she didn't like the party that she could call me at any time during the day or night and I would come and pick her up. She felt my unconditional love and prayer support. Time after time on the day of the party, our daughter would call and say she wasn't going. She didn't want to upset her peers so she asked her Dad if it was okay to say that he didn't approve of her going. She could make the decision that was best for her (with our help and advice) and everyone was pleased.

Teenagers need to learn to make decisions while still at home with their parent's guiding, loving, supporting and praying for them. And when these young people are old enough to leave home, they will amaze you with their maturity, level headedness and wisdom. There will be absolutely no evidence of wildness, rebellion, or immaturity.

My prayer life was really growing during these years. I spent an unbelievable amount of time praying the first years they were driving and especially their first winters to drive. God's counsel and guidance are original, unique, creative, loving and overcoming; so please call on Him for every situation and follow whatever He is saying to you. (Usually guidance comes as peaceful and wise thoughts impressed upon our minds as we focus on Him. Also, comforting words from our Bible reading will remain in our minds as if memorized, even though not actually memorized.)

Psalms 50:15 And call upon Me in the day of trouble; I shall rescue you, and you will honor me.

Moreover, praying about potential problems ahead of time will truly make life go much more smoothly. This is intercession and it is a lovely and important ministry.

Godly love and prayer support are very creative. I cannot put into words how important it is to grow in prayer. For just as there is a positive, creative force, there is also a negative, destructive force in the world. We can make problems far worse by arguing and condemning or we can "learn God's way" and return positive, gentle, loving, kind, encouraging and peacemaking words. I would suggest that you don't pray with doubt but visualize that Jesus is walking beside your child and protecting your child through these years. Truly growing in prayer is of great value and we'll learn how essential it is to pray the answer and not the problem.

Acts 12:5,7 & 11 So Peter was kept in the prison, but prayer for him was being made fervently by the church of God. [7] And behold, an Angel of the lord suddenly appeared, and a light shone in the cell; and he struck Peter's side and roused him, saying, "Get up quickly." And his chains fell off his hands. [11] And when Peter came to himself, he said, "now I know for sure that the Lord has sent forth His angel and rescued me from the hand of Herod and from all that the Jewish people were expecting."

Usually teenagers have a lot of needs (braces, bicycles, contact lenses, cars, car insurance, clothes, trips, college and so forth) and it may cause financial stress for the family. If the parents have upper management type jobs, they may also have job stress. Please discern that the stress is financial and job related and don't let it affect the marriage or the family. It is a time for the whole family to pull together and support and help each other with the finances.

During this time, I laid aside my self-will and put the needs of my family first. My wardrobe grew lean, my furniture older, and my house ready for paint; but I was young and healthy and there was plenty of time for these things after the college years were over. God blesses people who lay aside their own wills and put the Lord and their families first. He blesses them with maturity, Christlikeness, supernatural wisdom, grace, joy and on and on. The next chapters will go into greater detail about this concept.

Matthew 12:18-21 "Behold, My Servant whom I have chosen; My Beloved in whom My soul is well-pleased; I will put My Spirit upon Him, and He shall proclaim justice to the Gentiles. [19] He will not quarrel, nor cry out; nor will anyone hear his voice in the streets, [20] a battered reed he will not break off, and a smoldering wick He will not put out, until He leads justice to victory. [21] And in His Name the Gentiles will hope."

The Golden Rule says to do onto others first. This means to give love first.

Matthew 7:12 Therefore, however you want people to treat you, so treat them, for this is the Law and the Prophets.

We reap what we sow so please ask God to help you not be a negative and destructive force in your family. Always remember that praise and encouragement are very creative and of utmost importance to the developing identities of teenagers and will reap and sow marvelous results.

It is also excellent for mothers to only work part time, if it is possible, and be home when their teenagers come home from school for that is when the lines of communication are most open.

My oldest child graduated from college in three years and with honors. She is now married, a successful career woman, a terrific new mother, and doing very well.

My youngest child is working on his master's and doctorate degrees in physics and he has been on the dean's list. He has a beautiful personality and will be a great asset, in his special and unique way, to the world and to God. I am proud of both of them, and still I will always feel the need to cover them with prayer.

Now I did not talk about drugs or out of wedlock pregnancies because I am hoping that if you raise your child in a positive, loving, kind, giving, prayer-filled, church environment that these problems will be prevented. However, if you face these problems then you need more than ever to grow in your prayer lives and to hear from God what to do to overcome them.

The world is confused and does not know the answers. But if you grow close to God, He can help you to change first and then help you to help your family. Moreover, not only is our Lord able to help us through all problems (in His time), but He is also able to bring good out of them.

> **Romans 8:28** And we know that God causes all things to work together for good to those who love God, to those who are called according to His purpose.

Hannah Hurnard writes in "Hind's Feet on High Places" about the ABC's of love.

A   is accepting all things with joy.
B   is bearing the cost and forgiving.
C   is creative love thinking and praying.

Perhaps your child may pick up a deep and downcast attitude from school or friends. Then God may lead you to pray authority over it. You can pray and put their minds under the Lord's protection and ask the Lord to remove the darkness and confusion and replace it with His Light, Wisdom, Peace, Love, Joy and Presence - in the Name of Jesus! Authority prayers are powerful, they are binding and loosing prayers, and they are full of blessings.

> **Proverbs 31:28-31** Her children arise and call her blessed; her husband also, and he praises her: [29] Many women do noble things, but you surpass them all.
> [30] Charm is deceptive, and beauty is fleeting; but a woman who fears the Lord is to be praised. [31] Give her the reward she has earned, and let her works bring her

praise at the city gate. (NIV)

The next several chapters will teach us more about following Jesus our example. Remember also that at the end of this long path lay great victories and rewards. The world may not reward its hard workers but our Lord definitely does. Praise His Name!

11

JOSEPH

The story of Joseph is in the book of Genesis. It is a wonderful story of encouragement, and it is full of God's protection and rewards.

Joseph was one of the twelve sons of Jacob. He had ten older brothers, and only Benjamin was younger. His mother Rachel, was barren for many years and Joseph was an answer to her prayers. When he was seventeen years old, God gave Joseph two dreams in which his brothers and parents bowed down to him (Genesis, Chapter 37). His father loved Joseph and showed him favor. His older brothers were jealous of him and became even more so after his dreams. Consequently, the older brothers plotted to kill Joseph but the Lord was with him; and Reuben (the eldest) and Judah (the tribe Jesus came from) saved his life by selling him into slavery.

From the favorite son in a large family, Joseph now became the favorite servant in Potiphar's household. Joseph's master was an Egyptian officer and captain of Pharaoh's bodyguard. Moreover, the Lord was still with Joseph and caused all that he put his hands too, to prosper. Thus, Potiphar put all that he owned into Joseph's charge.

Genesis 39:1-6 Now Joseph had been taken down to Egypt; and Potiphar, an Egyptian officer of Pharaoh, the captain of the bodyguard, bought him from the Ishmaelite's, who had taken him down there. ² And the Lord was with Joseph, so he became a successful man. And he was in the house of his master, the Egyptian. ³ Now his master saw that the Lord was with him and how the Lord caused all that he did to prosper in his hand. ⁴ So Joseph found favor in his sight, and became his personal servant; and he made him overseer over his house, and all that he owned he put in his charge. ⁵ And it came about that from the time he made him overseer in his house, and over all that he owned, the Lord blessed the Egyptian's house on account of Joseph; thus, the Lord's blessing was upon all that he owned, in the house and in the field. ⁶ So he left everything he owned in Joseph's charge; and with him there he did not concern himself with anything except the food which he ate. Now Joseph was handsome in form and appearance.

During this time, Potiphar's wife desired Joseph, but he would not sin against God and he denied her. One day she grabbed his cloak as he fled, and she lied and said that he had attacked her. Her lies were believed and an innocent Joseph ended up in jail with the king's prisoners.

Even in prison Joseph was given favor, for the Lord was still with him, and he was put in charge of all the other prisoners.

Joseph was seventeen when he had his dreams and thirty years old when he was released from prison. Two years before he was freed from prison, the king's cupbearer and baker were sent to jail for offending the king. While they were in jail they both had disturbing dreams. With God's help, Joseph interpreted their dreams and he asked them to remember him when they were released. The interpretation of their dreams came true. The baker was killed and the cupbearer was restored to service - but they forgot about Joseph.

Joseph must have been terribly disappointed. He had done nothing wrong and he wanted so desperately to get out of jail and return home to his father. He had no choice when he was sold into slavery by his brothers. Neither did he have any choice when he was accused of lies and imprisoned. But now Joseph had a choice. He could go the natural way of bitterness, resentment and depression or he could go God's way.

God's way will never allow us to dwell upon the faults in others. So, Joseph turned his back on those thoughts and forced his mind to dwell on the Lord. Moreover, he found that the Lord was still with him and he began to hear God's voice. Now his father Jacob was a godly man, and his brothers were patriarchs of the twelve tribes of Israel, yet none of them heard God's voice of warning about the coming famine.

When the time came that Pharaoh had his frightening dream about the famine, the cupbearer remembered that Joseph could interpret dreams. Joseph was then brought from prison and with God's help he told Pharaoh about the seven good years and the seven lean years and how to store up grain and how to prepare for it.

God was continually with Joseph and he was raised up second to Pharaoh in the land. He had a powerful and hard training before he received his important ministry. Joseph came through these years a changed man. The trials in his life made him a Godly man; one who could safely and wisely handle power and lead his people with righteousness and not with arrogance, oppression, selfishness, or corruption.

Genesis 41:38-44 & 47-49 Then Pharaoh said to his servants, "Can we find a man like this, in whom is a divine spirit?" ³⁹ So Pharaoh said to Joseph, "Since God has informed you of all this, there is no one so discerning and wise as you are. ⁴⁰ You shall be over my house, and according to your command all my people shall do homage; only in the throne I will be greater than you". ⁴¹ And Pharaoh said to Joseph, "See I have set you over all the land of Egypt." ⁴² Then Pharaoh took off his signet ring from his hand, and put it on Joseph's hand, and clothed him in garments of fine linen, and put the gold necklace around his neck. ⁴³ And he had him ride in his second chariot; and they proclaimed before him, "Bow the knee!" And he set him over all the land of Egypt. ⁴⁴ Moreover, Pharaoh said to Joseph, "Though I am Pharaoh, yet without your permission no one shall raise his hand or foot in all the land of Egypt." ⁴⁷ And during the seven years of plenty the land brought forth abundantly. ⁴⁸ So he gathered all the food of these seven years which occurred in the land of Egypt, and placed the food in the cities; he placed in every city the food from its own surrounding fields. ⁴⁹ Thus Joseph stored up grain in great abundance like the sand of the sea, until he stopped measuring it, for it was beyond measure.

These verses show us how God was blessing and prospering Joseph. He became a ruler over Egypt and more and more Christ-like. Joseph had plenty of food during the famine and he fed his brothers and their families and even the Egyptian people - throughout the entire seven years. Joseph's life was now filled with power and wealth and blessings.

Joseph was given a wife and when the time came he named his first-born son, Manasseh. Manasseh means **God Has Made Me Forget All My Troubles**. When Joseph was blessed with another son, he named him Ephraim. Ephraim means **God Has**

Made Me Fruitful in the Land of My Affliction. Moreover, when Joseph's brothers came to him for food, he forgave them and said "It was not you, but God, who sent me before you to preserve lives."

Truly Jesus is our example of how to interact with people and how to live, and Joseph very much followed the example of Christ.

The gospels say over and over that God exalts the humble and those who exalt themselves will be humbled.

> **Luke 18:14** "I tell you, this man went down to his house justified rather than the other; for everyone who exalts himself shall be humbled, but he who humbles himself shall be exalted." (See also Matthew 23:12)

MY CHALLENGING TIMES

When I was young in the Lord and desiring to grow in Him, my family wanted to attend a church that I didn't want to go to. This church did not believe in the Holy Spirit and I did. We were all very active and supportive in this church and attended it for approximately five years; and I now look back on that time with fond memories as one of my greatest growing times in the Lord.

God taught me how to control my mind and overcome resentments. On Wednesday nights when someone insulted the Holy Spirit, God would give me Grace to smile and remain silent and just love them. But when I arrived home the grace was lifted and I became upset. Therefore, the following morning when my husband had left for work and the children were off to school, God would have me confess my resentments and then pray blessings on the people who had provoked me.

Matthew 5:44-45 "But I say to you love your enemies and pray for those who persecute you [45] in order that you may be sons of your Father who is in heaven; for He causes His sun to rise on the evil and the good, and sends rain on the righteous and the unrighteous.

I didn't want to go back to church, but I would go – holding out my right hand and imagining that Jesus was by my side and holding my hand.

Matthew 28:20b "And lo, I am with you always, even to the end of the age."

Always the Lord gave me grace to act mature and spiritual in church. But when I came home, the grace was lifted; and I would again be troubled and need to go to the Lord in prayer. When the leadership changed and the Lord opened a door for my family to move, I found that I didn't have a temper any more. I praise the Lord for that time and now look to the Lord in difficult times and expect His help, His teachings, and His doing something new and wonderful in my life.

If you are going through a difficult situation, you can call on God to be with you like He was with Joseph, and give you wisdom, patience and grace until He brings you into victory. Let God train you and change you so that you can properly and wisely handle all the blessings He wants to shower upon you. Praise the Lord!

Surely Joseph teaches us to be encouraged in hard and difficult times. We are to continue to trust in the Lord and to follow the beautiful examples of the people in the Bible. For after they had struggled for a little while, they were again lifted up and greatly rewarded. We can be like Moses (exiled in the Midian desert), David (chased by Saul and his armies), Joseph (slavery and imprisonment), Daniel (captured by Babylon and lion's den) and other such people who suffered rightly (Godly); and then were greatly exalted, honored, rewarded and needed. Their faith

was refined and became more precious than costly gold. Amen -
may it be so.

12

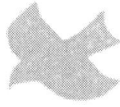

WALKING BY FAITH IN THE BUSINESS WORLD

What a testimony it has been getting our children through college with no savings, multiple job changes, lay-offs and no student loans. How we praise the Lord for His answers to prayer. During the last years of high school, I prayed for God to guide our children into the proper majors for them, for God to lead them to the university that was right for them, for finances, and for scholarships. I prayed hard because these are big decisions and I was very worried. A change in universities or majors can extend college time and increase finances.

I stepped down from the Women's Aglow ministry and prayed about a job a year before college started. I received a job with great benefits. The job was usually part time unless they wanted me full time. Even though I was low seniority, I never was laid off over the winter. This was unbelievable for that company and I can only thank the Lord for it. But even with raises, my yearly income wasn't covering their cars, car insurance, and college costs.

The scholarships were used up the first year of college. When our daughter had completed two years of college and our son was ready to enter college, my husband was laid off. I called on God, in prayer, and this is what the Lord said:

1 **Fear Not** - this is repeated many times in the Bible.

2 **Don't Complain or Blame.**

3 **Praise** - give thanks each day for what you have.

My husband's company laid off their whole production crew and had their main product built in Japan. My husband brought home a small product for me to build, assemble and package. He thought it would only last a couple of months. Then he took out a second mortgage and bought a small business.

Amazingly, my at-home job, or answer-to-prayer job, was booming. I also had my old job and was becoming exhausted. So, I sought the Lord in prayer for which job to give up. God usually doesn't speak out loud and I often get guidance from parts of scripture that stay in my mind (as if memorized though not actually memorized). Thus, when I seek God's direction, I turn to one or two bookmarks in my Bible and devotional and start reading. There was a verse in Deuteronomy 30, that stayed with me and said, I will bless what you put your hands too. Thus, eventually I felt led to take the bigger, at-home job with no benefits.

My sweet husband bought a television repair business and would never charge elderly, widow ladies what he should. What with taxes and overhead, the profits were small and I started praying for God to redeem our business loans. We knew some small business people that were terribly behind in income taxes and some that were going bankrupt. But God always says to look to him and trust. After a year, we put an advertisement in the paper and God instantly provided a buyer. At one point the negotiations came to a halt and the Lord gave me, through prayer, a simple new direction that satisfied everyone.

The key to problem solving is to simplify. This blows away the confusion. We give the Lord all the glory for providing a buyer and redeeming our business loans.

Romans 8:28 And we know that God causes all things to work together for good to those who love God, to those who are called according to His purpose.

Now, we both worked on the at-home job. Sometimes it was tremendously busy and at other times it was real slow. The company we built, assembled and packaged for went through several presidential changes and a couple of mergers. We never knew when this job would come to an end.

Time was passing and our oldest child graduated and then married. Our youngest child was halfway through college, when my husband accepted a great job the same week our at-home job was taken back into the company (following another merger).

We were so happy with the Lord's timing and the nice new job that was provided for my husband, just when we needed it. This learning to walk by faith is sort of strange. It demands frequent calling upon the Lord, abiding in Him, and a great deal of trust. Truly, one gradually comes to find a security in God that can be found in no one else. It is like what we read in the Bible:

Revelation 4:11 "Worthy art Thou, our Lord and our God, to receive glory and honor and power; for Thou didst create all things, and because of Thy will they existed, and were created."

However, five months later, my husband was laid off from his great job. I fasted three days (drinking juices) and prayed and really expected a job in two weeks. In two weeks, we received our at home job back, with the original pay, and there were lots of back orders to be filled. Looking back, this job (like manna) had always been there for us when we needed it. It was an answer to prayer from God, and the bulk of our support during the college years. Looking ahead, we never knew when orders would come in or if the job would last from month to month. But, surely our God is trustworthy. He who hears our prayers, also answers them - in His way and His time.

Abraham was the first man to learn to walk by faith, and it was pleasing to God. There is a beautiful growing in this walking by faith. At first, we are fearful and insecure and don't know if we can trust God. But as the years go by we come to know the Lord and to know that He is most trustworthy. At first it seems difficult to hear from God, but thankfully this also improves as the years go by. Oh, how special it is to grow in faith and bring God into every situation and be relaxed and mature and calm.

Romans 4:16-25 So God's blessings are given to us by faith as a free gift; we are certain to get them whether or not we follow Jewish customs if we have faith like Abraham's, for Abraham is the father of us all when it comes to these matters of faith. [17] That is what the Scriptures mean when they say that God made Abraham the father of many nations. God will accept all people in every nation who trust God as Abraham did. And this promise is from God himself, who makes the dead live again and speaks of future events with as much certainty as though they were already past. [18] So, when God told Abraham that he would give him a son who would have many descendants and become a great nation, Abraham believed God even through such a promise just couldn't come to pass! [19]And because his faith was strong, he didn't worry about the fact that he was too old to be a father, at the age of one hundred, and that Sarah his wife, at ninety, was also much too old to have a baby. [20] But Abraham never doubted. He believed God, for his faith and trust grew ever stronger, and he praised God for this blessing even before it happened. [21] He was completely sure that God was well able to do anything he promised. [22] And because of Abraham's faith God forgave his sins and declared him "not guilty." [23] Now this wonderful statement - that he was accepted and approved through his faith - wasn't just for Abraham's benefit. [24] It was for us, too, assuring us that God will accept us in the same way he accepted Abraham - when we believe the promises of God who brought back Jesus our Lord from the dead. [25] He died for our sins and rose again to make us right with God, filling us with God's goodness. (TLB)

Summer was supposed to be the slow season, in our job, but it wasn't. I needed finances to fly to Wisconsin, several times, as my father had inoperable cancer. What a summer! Whenever I was home, business was booming. And God had me everywhere at the right time. In Colorado to help my mother-in law when my husband's stepfather passed away, in Ohio to be with our daughter when our first grandchild was born, and back again to Wisconsin to be with my parents.

Our fathers were saved! Another prayer answered and God blessed and strengthened everyone and made them blessings. My father's hearing was restored towards the end and he said how restful and pleasant it was where he was going. My mother was blessed in a multitude of ways - with grace, food, flowers, company, cards, telephone calls, and emotionally and financially. It seemed like the entire county was a blessing to us.

Genesis 12:3a And I will bless those who bless you,

In addition to the other blessings and grace, God gave me the following steps to help overcome grief.

1 When loved ones are saved, even at the end, it isn't a permanent goodbye. You will see them again when it's

your time to go to heaven.

2 Standing strong and helping your family through this difficult time will bring a great deal of healing to you.

3 God has given you good memories. At first it is important to think on those good memories instead of the empty place in the family. Dwell on them until time passes and it's easier to look ahead.

How did we get through college costs, cars and car insurance for our children, lay-offs, job changes, our daughter's wedding, traveling and etc. successfully and without debts? Of course, it was the Lord. Moreover prayer, careful stewardship, hard work, and encouraging each other, helps too. It's important to go to God for guidance and then believe what He says for it will come true.

Matthew 8:13a And Jesus said to the centurion, "Go your way; let it be done to you as you have believed." (See also Matthew 9:29 and 15:28).

To walk in faith, we must give up self-pity. The old-nature is being put off and the new spiritual nature is emerging. The negative, complaining, depressed, fearful, old-nature becomes a barrier between you and God and cuts you off from His Presence and blessings. Even business leaders will hesitate to trust or promote angry, nervous and complaining employees.

As you walk by faith God will lead you to resist negative reports. The world usually gives negative reports and it is often the opposite of what the Lord says.

ONLY BELIEVE

Jairus came to Jesus to get Him to come home and heal his deathly, ill daughter. On the way home, a sick woman touched

Jesus and drew off His healing power. Did Jairus wonder if Jesus might not have any healing power left? Well, Jesus just looked at Jairus and said, "Do not be afraid any longer, only believe." They continued on their way to Jairus' house and the neighbors came and said, "Don't bother the Master any longer - she is dead." Jesus again looked at Jairus and said, "Only believe." As they arrived at the house, the funeral had started and people were wailing. Jesus once more looked at Jairus and said, "Only believe." If Jairus had believed those negative reports he would have let go of Jesus and lost his daughter. So, to succeed, let go of negative reports and not of God. (Mark 5:22-43)

It is important for us to give thanks, for this opens us up to receive more from God. Thanks, is the receiving attitude. It is also good to stand strong and courageous for our families during lay-offs and other hard times. It takes only one person to stand strong, believe, pray and support the whole family until the rough times pass - and how mature and Christ-like that is.

During one of the last slow times in our job, my husband was real worried, so I called on God for help and felt led to pray in tongues for several days (as much as I remembered), and another job opened up for my husband. I still may not know how secure these jobs are, but I trust God - that they will last as long as we need them to or until the Lord provides another job.

I Peter 2:6b And, the one who trusts in Him will never be put to shame. (NIV)

After these faith-building years we looked back and saw every bill paid, a terrific credit rating, no student loans, a savings account, and a start toward our retirement fund. Praise the Lord! Truly, asking for the Lord's help is a lovely and wise habit to get into.

In these days when some large businesses are restructuring

and laying off, we need to go to God. He alone knows the future and will give us discernment, balance, wisdom, and guidance. He alone is a solid rock; secure, unchanging, powerful and wise. Moreover, God may lead us to pray for sales to open in Jesus' Name. It is possible that businesses may stand and continue and be spared bankruptcies as we grow in the Lord and learn to pray with authority and blessings.

I Timothy 2:1-2 First of all, then, I urge that entreaties and prayers, petitions and thanksgivings, be made on behalf of all men, ²for kings and all who are in authority, in order that we may lead a tranquil and quiet life in all godliness and dignity.

When you are trying to walk by faith and you pick up anger, depression, criticizing and etc. from the people around you, just ask God to be over it and remove all those old-nature attitudes from you. Don't condemn yourself, just discern that you picked it up and confess it to the Lord in prayer.

Follow the Lord on the path of trust and faith.
If mountains (problems) arise on the road before you, God will take you beyond them and it will be as if they weren't even there. For truly your God is more powerful than the things that you see.

Oh how we need to walk with God in the fruits of the Spirit (love, peace, joy, kindness and etc.), even in stressful times. Thus, we will find ourselves growing in faith and learning to depend on the Lord, and behold - we become new and better people after the stressful times have passed. That is how the famous people of the Bible received blessings, honors and rewards. They let go of their own way and lost their lives to find life – life as kings, and leaders, and great, Godly, wise, and blessed men.

The Lord has seen us through job lay-offs (more than once), through college years, through financial worries, through a child's wedding, through deaths of parents, through grandchildren and even through health problems. Truly in all these things we have seen victory after victory. Praise God! He is able! He is enough! And verily He rewards those who turn to Him and trust in Him.

May He add blessing upon blessing and grant to those who seek His help a double portion of prosperity and joy. Amen.

13

SPIRITUAL WIVES - SPIRITUAL PEOPLE

The spiritual life is extremely different from the natural, logical life and point of view. Elijah is a good example of how the spiritual way doesn't make sense and doesn't seem logical to our normal way of thinking.

In I Kings 17, there was a drought and famine in the land. At first, Elijah was by a brook and the ravens brought him food, but eventually the brook dried up and God told him to arise and go dwell with a widow in Zarephath. When Elijah arrived at the widow's place, she was preparing her last meal for herself and her son. Now, it doesn't make sense to be sent to people who are supposed to feed you through the remainder of the famine and find that they are on their last meal. It also didn't make sense to the widow to see this mighty man of God, who had been connected with God's miracle-working power, ask for some of their last meal before they had tasted it. But she obeyed and gave Elijah some food, first, and God did a miracle; her bowl of flour and jar of oil did not run out until the famine was over.

Matthew 16:25 "For whoever wishes to save his life shall lose it; but whoever loses his life for My sake shall find it.

This scripture basically says that if we let go of our own way and follow God's way - we will find life. It is the reverse of what the world tells us.

God very much wants us to be kind to all the members of our family. God blesses the righteous, and He knows that we reap what we sow. Thus, even if we face anger, the Lord wants us to return kindness. It is amazing that we have the power to be either creative or destructive. If we give negative words, we can increase such attitudes in the people around us and receive disastrous words back.

In a family disagreement, the world's advice is to argue and get rid of your tension. But this only seems to reinforce and enlarge the problem and eventually people end up with divided homes and no hope for solving their problems.

James 4:7-8 Submit yourselves, then, to God. Resist the devil, and He will flee from you. [8] **Come near to God and he will come near to you**. Wash your hands, you sinners, and purify your hearts, you double-minded. (NIV)

However, if we turn to God, He will help us to concentrate on the good in the family and reinforce and enlarge that. Words are tremendously creative or destructive. Proverbs 18:21 says that there is life or death in the tongue. We are created in God's image in this area of speaking creatively or destructively.

As we turn to God for His help, one of the first things He suggests is to be rested up. There are numerous social events that leave us drained and exhausted. God will guide us when to say no, and also which events are important to the family. It is almost impossible to speak nice, kind, loving and encouraging words when one is over tired. But praise the Lord, nothing is impossible for God, so call on Him for extra help and grace when you are working late.

When our children were teenagers, they were only involved with school and church activities. They played sports with their friends, but didn't have time for competitive sports or youth clubs. Children are different and some events will be important to them and others will only be time consuming and tire them out. Our children were in advanced classes, band and school newspaper; and they needed extra time to study and time just to relax.

I believe that only God is perfect. I know that I'm not and yet God still loves me. I want to accept my family just as they are and give them love. I want all of us to be mature and be givers and not takers. If we are the first one in our family to lay aside self-will and give love, God will help us and bless us. Eventually the rest of the family will follow and become spiritual people, manifesting the fruits of the Spirit (Galatians 5:22-23).

I have mentioned the fruits of the Spirit many times, but perhaps I should include one of the opposite scriptures on the fruits of the old-nature.

Galatians 5:19-21a Now the deeds of the flesh are evident, which are: immorality, impurity, sensuality, [20] idolatry, sorcery, enmities, strife, jealousy, outbursts of anger, disputes, dissensions, factions, [21a] envying, drunkenness, carousing, and things like these, of which I forewarn you.

Love is truly an important quality in our relationships with God and with other people. Love is the message of the Cross. Our Bible has a profound definition of love:

I Corinthians 13:4-8a Love is patient, love is kind, and is not jealous; love does not brag and is not arrogant, [5] does not act unbecomingly; it does not seek its own, is not provoked, does not take into account a wrong suffered, [6] does not rejoice in unrighteousness, but rejoices with the truth; [7] bears all things, believes all things, hopes all things, endures all things. [8a] Love never fails.

The first three verses in this chapter say that love is much more excellent than prophecy, faith, generosity, and the rest of the spiritual gifts. The Bible tells us that love covers a multitude of sins and that the greatest commandments are to love God and others. And God is love, so first we go to God to receive love and then we give it out.

A **Prophecy** for wives, mothers, and spiritual people.
My beloved child:
I saw you lead your husband to church.
I know when you teach your children about Me, their Lord.
I hear your prayers for your family.
I know your hours and hours of intercession.
Surely you hold your family together.
You even go out to work and help support them.
Time after time you laid self-will aside and put God and your family first.
 I see you serving Me in your neighborhood and church and serving your family at home.
Yes, I see your self-will laid aside and your family and your Lord put first.
And I, says the Lord your God, "Will bless you and honor you and reward you. And I will bless your family through you and I will give you the heart and mind of Christ."

As I write this book, new revelation comes from our precious Lord. I always knew that God would help all those who turn to Him - through their hard times. He will also protect them and be with them until victory appears, no matter how long it takes. But I never realized how much He is changing us in the process - turning us from fearful, old nature people into wise, strong, creative, and righteous people who are able to handle power and leadership, successfully.

II Corinthians 3:18 But we all, with unveiled face beholding as a mirror the glory of the Lord, are being transformed into the same image from glory to glory, just as from the Lord, the Spirit. (NIV)

We eventually come to understand what Paul meant when he said he could do all things through Christ who strengthened him.

Philippians 4:13 I can do all things through Him who strengthens me.

Paul was high with joy, enthusiasm, excitement and life when he said that. So, let us abide with God that we might be fruitful.

John 15:5 I am the vine, you are the branches; he who abides in Me, and I in him, he bears much fruit; for apart from Me you can do nothing.

It is God whom we praise. It is God who helps us, anoints us and gives us supernatural wisdom and grace. God is all in all. Man's will and attempts apart from God, will eventually fail.

Acts 5:38-39 And so in the present case, I say to you, stay away from these men and let them alone, for if this plan or action should be of men, it will be overthrown, [39] but if it is of God, you will not be able to overthrow them; or else you may even be found fighting against God.

God wants us to have healthy minds and a good way of doing so is to obey His Bible and leave vengeance up to Him. We can choose to let go of self-pity and fearful, negative emotions that cut us off from God and bring ill health and failure. We can call on God for help to walk with Him and prosper at whatever we put our hands, too.

Deuteronomy 30:8-10&19-20a You will again obey the Lord and follow all His commands I am giving you today. [9] Then the Lord your God will make you most prosperous in all the work of your hands and in the fruit of your womb, the young of your livestock and the crops of your land. The Lord will again delight in you and make you prosperous, just as He delighted in your ancestors, [10] if you obey the Lord your God and keep His commands and decrees that are written in this Book of the Law and turn to the Lord your God with all your heart and with all your soul. [19] This day I call heaven and earth as witnesses against you that I have set before you life and death, blessings and curses. Now choose life, so that you and your children may live [20] and that you may love the Lord your God, listen to His voice, and hold fast to Him. For the Lord is your life. (NIV)

This whole chapter is beautiful and shows us how to walk in restoration and blessings or in increasing problems. Leviticus 26 is similar to Deuteronomy 28 - 30 and reinforces these same teachings. Thankfully, with age comes wisdom and we realize how weak and pitiful and faulty are our attempts at controlling our own lives. Likewise, we see how goodness and power and wisdom belong with our Creator. Hopefully, we will all turn to Him and ever so gradually allow the Lord His rightful place in our lives.

The Almighty, Creator, Father, God is amazing and awesome. He wants this book to take people beyond positive thinking and into a relationship with Himself. Yes, like He was with the people in the Bible, God is with us in our stressful times (just talk to Him and you will know He is near). And He will stay with us and help us until these times pass and blessings come. But God is doing even more than that - He is renewing our minds and changing us. These minds, now, are close to God and take God's Presence with us wherever we go. We find that we see situations through God's eyes and that our words and prayers are heard and answered.

Truly, spiritual people are heavenly people to be around. They frequently replace their thoughts with God's thoughts and they never dwell on people's faults. They feed their minds on songs, thanksgiving, praise, worship, and true, just, lovely and pure things (Philippians 4:8). Such food in their minds produce words that are powerful and blessed. They see good things in people and bless instead of criticize. They are full of prayer and forgiveness and the Bible. Truly, all their problems seem to turn into blessings. Yes, happy are they and our God can help us to become just like them. Praise the Lord! And many are the promises for the righteous.

Reference:
Please see Walking Among the Unseen by Hannah Hurnard for a whole book on this subject.

14

ANOINTED LEADERS

God is constantly training leaders. This is a continually evolving process as His people learn about Him, and grow up in Him, and become strong and balanced. Those who prophesy tell us that there is a harvest of baby Christians coming into the church today, and that they need to be parented.

Truly, mature leaders know the Bible and they know their Lord and they love Him. They treat people like God treats them - with understanding, forgiveness, counsel, power, love, hope and so much more. Such leaders ask and depend upon God's help, and as they do God's will and wait upon God's timing, they have anointing and success. They are with God and He is with them. These people spend a lot of time with the Lord and have learned to hear His voice.

John 10:27 My sheep hear My voice, and I know them, and they follow Me.

Awhile back, I attended a Bible study and one evening a young couple came in late and quietly sat down. After the Bible study concluded, we had prayer-time and the teacher prayed for the new people. While he was praying, I saw a vision of a cup and a scripture came to mind, with the word "cup" in it.

Psalm 23:5 Thou dost prepare a table before me in the presence of my enemies; Thou has anointed my head with oil; my cup overflows.

After mentioning the vision and reading the scripture; I said, "God prepares a table for you (feeds and teaches you) in the midst of enemies. These enemies could be financial stress or anything that is difficult. It is in the midst of these difficult times that God will **anoint** you and eventually your cup will overflow." Everyone was silent and seemed to get new and personal meaning out of that verse. When the meeting was over, the young couple asked me to go out to their van. The young man said, "See, it is full of our furniture. I planned on going AWOL tonight, but what you said changed my mind." The Lord had led him to that Bible study and those words changed his mind and with new determination he returned to his base.

I never saw that young couple again, either before or after that evening. Yet, there are times when I still think of them and say a prayer for God's grace and abundant blessings upon their lives.

Discernment is vital to leaders, especially when discouraged, defeated, perhaps disobedient, and possibly even manipulating people come to us or call us. We can listen, encourage, give something from God's Word, be open to spiritual gifts, and pray. We are just the one who prays. God is the important one. He is the answerer of prayers.

Many people come to leaders for prayer. What a great pleasure it is to lay hands on these people and pray for them. As we focus on the Lord and attempt to speak His words of blessing, we see a tremendous transformation taking place as the prayer ends. We look in amazement at a face that is now radiant and smiling, and cheeks that have tears of joy running down them. Surely God is awesome and indescribable feelings of joy fill us vessels of the Lord.

After years of hearing people's problems (some that are magnified), God will tell leaders to see Him as the burden bearer and to come away and rest awhile. God wants us to be refreshed and restored. He is the Lord of our lives and all other things, including ministry, are underneath him. We don't need to do everything that is asked of us. God only anoints what He asks us to do. Moreover, leaders should desire to help people mature and then they should decrease so that the Lord can increase in the lives of others.

John 3:30 He must increase, but I must decrease.

Jesus, still is our example, today. He is unchanging, His work on the cross still saves us, and the Holy Spirit is still given without measure. Jesus seems to take us beyond our ideas of ministry - to simply taking God's Presence with us and being free to do the Father's will. Jesus' example of a prophet goes beyond Old Testament prophets. Study about Jesus in the gospels and learn about God. He was never pushy, domineering, judgmental, or condemning (Mark 10:42-45.) Those He healed were never frightened by His power. He freely gives love, grace, life, comfort, truth, advice and freedom. Follow the gentle, humble, yet powerful Jesus and grow up in Him. For an immature Christian is like a slave, not free or able to inherit the promises.

Galatians 4:1 Now I say, as long as the heir is a child, he does not differ at all from a slave although he is owner of everything.

Hearing from God is important to leaders and to everyone. Remember Moses and all the murmuring people with him in the wilderness. Each time they ran out of water or came to bitter water, the people would panic and want to run away (back to

Egypt). But a leader trusts God, goes to God in prayer, and hears what to do. For each situation, Moses was instructed to do something different; put a tree in the bitter water, strike a rock and water would come out, and so on. Also, great battles were won in the Old Testament by going to God and doing what He said. Joshua, Gideon, David, Elisha, and others won great victories with God's supernatural wisdom and strategy.

The way we react to a problem will show whether we are a leader or not. Do we fall into fear or anger or hopelessness, and stay there, or do we go directly to God and the Bible and Prayer and seek His help and guidance?

What a short cut it is to hear from God in problems. The world, committees, Christian gatherings and a multitude of voices can bring confusion. But as we turn to the Lord and His Word and Prayer - we may find a scripture put in our minds. It may say something like, "Fear not, I will take care of you" and great peace comes and the problems start to fade.

Of course, we need to slow down from the rushing of the world, to hear from God and to seek time alone with Him.

Psalm 46:10a He says "Be still and know that I am God," (NIV)

A friend asked me what to do if a person waits and still doesn't hear from God. Well, then it is always safe to do the teachings of the Bible, for that is God's Words. Deuteronomy 28, tells us that those who obey God's teachings will prosper and the rebellious will fail. So then, it is always wise to yield to the wisdom of His Words and trust them. Joshua 1:8 and the first Psalm tell us that those who abide in the Bible will be blessed. Truly, knowledge of the Bible is what separates a Baby Christian from an Adult Christian - for knowledge of the Scripture is also knowledge of God.

The Holy Spirit lives in us and makes our bodies, churches - yea even temples. Being in the Bible sets our minds free and fills, renews and helps make our minds righteous. Anointed powerful leaders have righteous minds.

> **John 8:31-32** Jesus therefore was saying to those Jews who had believed Him, "If you abide in My word, then you are truly disciples of Mine; [32] and you shall know the truth, and the truth shall make you free."

> **Philippians 4:8** Finally, brethren, whatever is true, whatever is honorable, whatever is right, whatever is pure, whatever is lovely, whatever is of good repute, if there is any excellence and if anything worthy of praise, let your mind dwell on these things.

We are channels to speak His words. God wants to give His glory to us so that He can be manifested on earth.

∗   ∗   ∗

Around 1985, on New Year's Eve, I had a dream that said there are a lot of sickness spirits coming into the world today, and we need to abide close to God to be kept safe. The dream also said that abiding meant spending time in the Bible.

If a person feels that Satan is attacking them, then they need to stand still, and fill up with the Lord, and He will fight for them.

> **II Chronicles 20:15,17** and he said, "Listen, all Judah and the inhabitants of Jerusalem and King Jehoshaphat: thus says the Lord to you, 'do not fear or be dismayed because of this great multitude, for the battle is not yours but Gods. [17]You need not fight this battle; station yourselves, stand and see the salvation of the Lord on your behalf, O Judah and Jerusalem.' Do not fear or be dismayed; tomorrow go out to face them, for the Lord is with you."

I Chronicles 14:14-15 And David inquired again of God and God said to him. You shall not go up after them; circle around behind them, and come at them in front of the balsam trees. [15] And it shall be when you hear the sound of marching in the tops of the balsam trees, then you shall go out to battle, for God will have gone out before you to strike the army of the Philistines.

I Samuel 17:47 and that all this assembly may know that the Lord does not deliver by sword or by spear; for the battle is the Lord's and He will give you into our hands.

*   *   *

Sometimes I see anointed people trying to overcome minor health problems that linger on.

II Corinthians 12:9a And He has said to me, "My grace is sufficient for you, for power is perfected in weakness.

Are they in advanced classes with the Lord? Are they learning to battle spirits in heavenly places (Ephesians 6:12-13)? Are they learning to lean heavily on the Lord and to discern and to know God's authority? Will these people come out of this with power to pray for healings and miracles for the many? According to scripture, we can do the works that Christ did. But, what a lot of work God must do in us to bring us to that point. However, the Lord says to never let in discouragement. There is a purpose for everything and a training and rewards.

Whatever the Lord is doing, illness becomes a blessing as it draws people even closer to Him. It is lovely to see these people filled with God and overflowing with His love and Presence and Words. Moreover, they have the privilege of entering a very high

82

ministry - that of prayer and intercession. I think this is especially what old age is meant to be. They have the time to draw very close to God and the refreshing that fills them will overflow to the younger, hurried, busy world around them. Though it is best not to wait until we are old to become such prayers and blessers. For verily, the world of today is sending up a cry and a demand to God for anointed and Godly leaders.

*   *   *

I find myself frequently asking the Lord to be in control of situations. He alone, knows the future and knows what is best for all, so I ask Him to be in control and to open or close doors. Yes, most often lately, I'm praying for God's will and not my own and I'm seeing many, many lovely answers to prayer - what a paradox.

How hard it seems to learn to relinquish our own way of handling problems. To relinquish fear, anger, hopelessness, human reasoning, striving and struggling. Yes, to relinquish self (surrender, cease striving) and call on God for greater wisdom, greater help and greater power. Astonishing as it seems, yet it is true, that the Lord can take better care of us than we can of ourselves.

It is amazing how simple problems become when they are viewed from God's perspective. Why it's a chance for God to do something great, reveal more of Himself, teach us, mature us and test our faith so that He can reward it.

FAITH:
1 Sometimes God tests His children's FAITH to see if they trust Him. We see this in the wilderness wanderings with Moses.
2 FAITH is reckoned to us as righteousness. Abraham, the

83

father of all who walk by faith, teaches us this. Romans 4:3

3 The righteous shall live by FAITH. Habakkuk and Galatians 3:11

4 FAITH pleases God. Hebrews 11:6

5 FAITH is rewarded. Hebrews 11:6

6 Faith comes by reading the Bible. Romans 10:17. So faith comes from hearing, and hearing by the word of God.

7 FAITH praises!

Habakkuk 3:17-19 Though the fig tree should not blossom, and there be no fruit on the vines, though the yield of the olive should fail, and the fields produce no food, though the flock be cut off from the fold, and there be no cattle in the stalls, [18] yet I will exult in the Lord. I will rejoice in the God of my salvation. [19] the Lord is my strength, and he has made my feet like hinds' feet, and makes me walk on high places.

Acts 16:24-26 and he, having received such a command, threw them into the inner prison, and fastened their feet in the stocks. [25] but about midnight Paul and Silas were praying and singing hymns of praise to God, and the prisoners were listening to them; [26] and suddenly there came a great earthquake, so that the foundations of the prison house were shaken; and immediately all the doors were opened, and everyone's chains were unfastened.

We are also justified by faith (Romans 5:1), and faith is many more things. I find this chapter to be beyond me, but as you walk and talk with the Lord, He will bless you and teach you what He wants you to know.

Often times, we just need to stand strong, and trust and pray for others, until their victory comes. For problems are often like Daniel's lion's den; if Daniel had refused to spend the night in the lion's den, a great many people wouldn't have known the greatness of God. But thankfully Daniel trusted God and entered the lion's den and came out safely, and all the people heard about it and rejoiced in such an awesome God.

II Corinthians 2:14 But thanks be to God who always leads us in His triumph in Christ, and manifests through us the sweet aroma of the knowledge of Him in every place.

Today, the Holy Spirit is needed more than ever. It is the power part of the Godhead and yet it is so very gentle that it's symbol is a dove. Anointed leaders will be a similar paradox of gentleness and power.

Isaiah 61:1-4a "The Spirit of the Lord God is upon me, because the Lord has anointed me to bring good news to the afflicted; He has sent me to bind up the brokenhearted, to proclaim liberty to captives, and freedom to prisoners; [2] to proclaim the favorable year of the Lord, and the day of vengeance of our God; to comfort all who mourn, [3] to grant those who mourn in Zion, giving them a garland instead of ashes, the oil of gladness instead of mourning, the mantle of praise instead of a spirit of fainting. So, they will be called oaks of righteousness, the planting of the Lord, that He may be glorified. [4a] Then they will rebuild the ancient ruins, they will raise up the former devastations, and they will repair the ruined cities.

Surely, like a vision I had in church recently, leaders walked on a bridge over troubled waters. The bridge was like the golden gate bridge. It was long and beautiful and it represented a humble walk, close to God. The troubled waters represent a multitude of peoples, crying out for help. Truly, wise leaders will point the people to God, and teach them about Him, and how He can help them be overcomers.

John 16:33 "I have told you these things, so that in Me you may have peace. In this world, you will have trouble. But take heart! I have overcome the world." (NIV)

Behold now, your Lord, the One Who Loves you. Behold how Jesus stayed free of man's ministries to go where the Father wanted Him to go and to speak the Father's Words. Behold the early Christians and the vast amount of time they gave to prayer, so that when My Spirit led them out it could do so with signs and wonders. Behold Me and be refreshed. Behold My righteousness and power and know that whatever you need I will supply. Behold My right hand stretched out to carry you along the paths of life. And behold My glory and become one with Me.

15

VISIONS OF GROWTH

The dream had awakened me. The next day it continued - strong and vivid, in my mind. Finally, I decided to pray about it. Maybe the dream had meaning and purpose. Little did I know that a series of visions would come over the next several years, and continue from that dream, and tell about Christian growth.

John 16:13 "But when He, the Spirit of truth comes, He will guide you into all truth; for He will not speak on His own initiative, but whatever He hears, He will speak; and He will disclose to you what is to come.

This **Dream** (or **Vision** in the night as the prophets called them) was about the place where we lived just before moving into our present house. We have been in our present home for approximately seventeen years. Prior to that, we rented a duplex. In the dream, I could see the inside of the duplex and it was empty of furniture. Also in the dream, the floor boards were rotten and sagging in between all the floor joists. Even the bottom of the door frame was loose and wobbly. We lived near the end of the street and only one family lived to our right and many families lived on our left. Then in my dream, I took our two young children in the car and attempted to go buy food, but I kept getting lost and kept needing to stop and ask for directions.

I asked the Lord what all this meant and slowly the word "foundation" came to my mind. I had not been brought up in a church and was unsaved. The only foundation is in Christ Jesus. The one family to our right went to church and all the families on the left, didn't. The rotten, sagging foundations (ours and those on the left) were weak, unsafe, insecure and should have been condemned. Truly this is the condition of unbelievers' lives. Moreover, when we don't know the Lord we are lost and in need of real food - the Word of God.

> **Matthew 4:4** But He answered and said, "It is written, man shall not live on bread alone, but on every word that proceeds out of the mouth of God. "

This vision was symbolic. The building was in good shape when we lived there. It was in that place that I started seeking the Lord, reading the Bible, learning to pray, and even doing correspondence Bible studies on salvation, through the Billy Graham organization. I prayed a prayer of salvation and started the building of a strong foundation (relationship with God) in that duplex.

> **Matthew 7:24-27** "Therefore everyone who hears these words of Mine, and acts upon them, may be compared to a wise man, who built his house upon the rock.
> 25 "And the rain descended, and the floods came, and the winds blew, and burst against that house; and yet it did not fall for it had been founded upon the rock.
> 26 "And everyone who hears these words of Mine, and does not act upon them, will be like a foolish man, who built his house upon the sand. 27 "And the rain descended, and the floods came, and the winds blew, and burst against that house; and it fell, and great was its fall."

Everyone can let go of their shaky foundations and go to Jesus and build strong ones. Truly the gospels show that our Lord is addressed by many titles. In addition, He also gives Himself names, such as the following scripture reveals:

> **John 6:35** Jesus said to them, "I am the Bread of Life; he who comes to Me shall not hunger, and he who believes in Me shall never thirst."

Sometime later, a **Second Vision** came. This vision was of a dining room. The dining room was long and dark and filled with costly furniture. The huge table and chairs were of nice mahogany wood. The drapes were a rich, thick brocade and they were closed.

At the time, I thought we might be moving into a new house and this furniture would be left for us. But why would the long, dark, elegant room seem like a tunnel? Nevertheless, the Lord would be with us and teach us during this time.

> **Psalm 23:4-5** Even though I walk through the valley of the shadow of death, I will fear no evil; for Thou art with me; Thy rod and Thy staff, they comfort me. [5] Thou dost preparest a table before me in the presence of my enemies; Thou has anointest my head with oil; my cup runneth over. (KJV)

This was a time when the old nature was being put to death (yea, even crucified) and the new spiritual nature was starting to emerge. As a family, we wholeheartedly bought Bibles and attended church, church activities and numerous Bible studies. Suddenly, we were hungry to learn about the Lord. Our lives were busy, full, enjoyable, and closely knit together.

Frequently, in this country, the wife and children start going to church first. Never pressure the husband to attend, for that is ineffective and never the way of the Spirit. Just simply come home from church overflowing with life, enthusiasm, and joy and soon the husband will be coming along. For surely, the fruits of the Spirit are salt and light and a mighty attraction.

The **Third Vision** was of a family room. This room was square and sunny and the house was halfway up the side of a mountain. There were many windows and the sunlight was pouring in. The furniture looked like new, and the wood was light in color. The upholstered part was yellow, with a floral design. Again, I wondered if we were moving into this sunny mountain home with a roomful of new furniture, waiting for us.

In the vision, I saw myself trying to get unpacked and everything done before my husband came home from work and the children from school. But the neighbor children (pre-school age) kept coming over. They wanted to be with me and hear me laugh and talk about the Lord. In this vision, there was a man working on the kitchen faucet and he also loved the peaceful, serene atmosphere.

This vision also had a child playing outside and he hurt his hand on some wild weeds. He came crying to me and with a hug and a prayer he was instantly healed. Moreover, some door to door sales people were given a cup of cold water and rested for a moment while something gentle and loving was said about the Lord.

Matthew 10:42 "And whoever in the name of a disciple gives to one of these little ones even a cup of cold water to drink, truly I say to you he shall not lose his reward."

This was a happy time of fellowshipping with the Lord, spending lots of time in the Bible and prayer, overflowing with Godly and encouraging words, and reaping and sowing a multitude of blessings.

Ephesians 5:18b-20 Be filled with the Spirit, [19] speaking to one another in psalms and hymns and spiritual songs, singing and making melody with your heart to the Lord; [20] always giving thanks for all things in the name of our Lord Jesus Christ to God even the Father.

The **Fourth Vision** of a house was a long, white, two-story building with an A-frame roof. This house was old, in perfect condition, immaculately landscaped and in the country, because it had a gravel driveway. Because of its size, it seemed like it could have been a country church at one time.

During this time, my husband and I were deacon and deaconess. We also had people over for Bible study, prayer for everyone's needs, encouragement, food, and to uplift the Lord. Like a country church, we were sharing the Lord with a small group of people.

A year later, I saw this long, white, two-story, A-frame house change. This **Fifth Vision** came while I was alone and in prayer. An addition was added onto both ends of the house (advancing forward), a cross was added on top of the central front area, and pavement and new landscaping surrounded the whole building.

I Corinthians 3:16 Do you not know that you are a temple of God, and that the Spirit of God dwells in you?

Now, we were to be the Lord's temple in the city and more people would come to us and seek the Lord. At work and in Full Gospel Businessmen's organizations, my husband was often approached for prayer, advice and encouragement. I served in Women's Aglow organizations and my phone seemed to ring off the hook with a multitude of ladies needing understanding, encouragement, scripture and prayer. As I was led into leadership positions, my heart cried out to the Lord to help the many, many hurting people in my neighborhood and other areas.

*　　*　　*

Even in the book of Job, we see that real help comes from God. Yes, Job's friends came, but they weren't much help. Job needed prayer, God's presence, and a word from God - not the analyzing, criticizing, and human reasoning that the world and Job's friends gave.

Psalm 121:1-2 I will lift up my eyes to the mountains; from whence shall my help come? [2] My help comes from the Lord, who made heaven and earth.

A **Sixth Vision** came after the foundation, dining room, sunny family room, small country church and larger city-church visions. The sixth and I thought the final vision in this series of visions was of a "citadel". There was a huge seacoast and a narrow path going up a high mountainous-cliff. The path led up to a small building at the top of the cliff. Then the path went down the other side of the mountain and into a valley where a city was nestled. A small building, sitting on the narrow path and at the top the mountain, was the citadel. No enemies could come into the city except by way of the citadel; and one soldier, with many weapons, could keep the whole city safe. The word citadel was strong in my mind and so I went to the dictionary for a definition.

CITADEL:
1 A fortress on a commanding height for defense of a city.
2 A fortified place; stronghold.
3 A refuge; place of retreat.

Isaiah 62:6 "On your walls O Jerusalem, I have

appointed watchmen; all day and all night they will never keep silent, you who remind the Lord, take no rest for yourselves:

I kept thinking that one prayer warrior (intercessor) could keep a whole city safe. Prayer warriors can even discern potential problems and call on God's help and grace, ahead of time, for smoother sailing. Praise the Lord. Truly, I am just a prayer warrior for my family, church, street, pastors, work, relatives, organizations I attend, the president, and whatever else the Lord brings to mind. However, this is pleasing to the Lord and He likens it to a city.

*   *   *

Chapter six of the book of Ephesians talks about the armor of God. Every time I read it, I get more out of it. Now of course everyone who is saved can wear the "Helmet of Salvation."

The "Breastplate of Righteousness" covers the heart area. Those whose hearts are right with God can wear the breastplate. These hearts have sought the Lord, and received cleansing from evil, unforgiveness, anger, bitterness, deceit, pride, jealousy, and so forth.

The "Shield of Faith" protects us from the enemies' arrows. Those who trust like Moses have the shield of faith. Many Old Testament characters knew about the shield of faith. But like Gideon, they had to go to God and hear what He said before they were brave enough to face vast armies with only three hundred men (Judges, Chapters 6 & 7). Faith covers and protects us like a shield, and stops evil from getting through, as we focus our minds on the Lord and His Words.

The "Sword of the Spirit" is the Word of God. God's Word is an offensive weapon. Being in the Bible is the best place to hear from God. Like Moses, David and etc., we can go to God in problems and seek His "Still small voice."

I Kings 19:11-13 And He said, go forth, and stand upon the mount before the Lord. And, behold, the Lord passed by, and a great strong wind rent the mountains, and brake in pieces the rocks before the Lord; but the Lord was not in the wind: and after the wind an earthquake; but the Lord was not in the earthquake: [12] And after the earthquake a fire, but the Lord was not in the fire: and after the fire a still small voice [13] and it was so, when Elijah heard it, that he wrapped his face in his mantle, and went out, and stood in the entering in of the cave. And, behold, there came a voice unto him, and said, What doest thou here, Elijah" (KJV)

Hearing from the Lord, was how David rescued his family and all his men's families, when they were captured by the Amalekites. David's men were angry and about to stone him before David sought the Lord, and obeyed, and turned disaster into victory (I Samuel Chapter 30). There were other times also that David strengthened himself in the Lord and inquired of the Lord, what he should do.

1 Chronicles 14:14-15 And David inquired again of God, and God said to him, "You shall not go up after them; circle around behind them, and come at them in front of the balsam trees. [15] And it shall be when you hear the sound of marching in the tops of the balsam trees, then you shall go out to battle, for God will have gone out before you to strike the army of the Philistines.

Truly, Jesus seems to be all the different pieces of armor. He is both in us and around us. We need only talk to Him and ask His help. For verily He is our glory and power and life and all in all!

Praying in the Spirit is mentioned at the end of the armor scripture. I suppose that this also means praying in tongues. I often forget to stir up this gift and pray in tongues, but truly I tell you that this is a powerful form of prayer.

TONGUES:
1 Edifies and builds us up.
2 Increases our faith.
3 Renews and restores our minds.
4 Helps us become worshipers and lifts us up into the heavenlies.
5 Readies us for service.
6 Allows God's Words and power to flow through us.
7 Helps us receive God's blessings.
8 Intercedes for others.
9 Brings discernment and revelation.
10 Does spiritual warfare.
11 Brings victory when nothing else works.
12 Fairly continuous tongues helped bring us a new job.
13 Fairly continuous tongues help us receive and keep healings.
14 Moreover, this prayer in the Spirit makes your day go better.

Tongues is a part of prayer, and Prayer and the Bible is what this relationship (abundant life) is all about.

John 10:10 "The thief comes only to steal, and kill, and destroy; I came that they might have life, and might have it abundantly.

The Six Vision Were:

1 **Crumbling Foundation** - needing salvation and Christ the only secure foundation.
2 **Long Dining Room** - feeding on the Word and joining Bible studies.

3 **Sunny Family Room** - pleasant family togetherness in church activities.
4 **Small Country Church** - ministering to a few.
5 **Larger City Church** - ministering to more.
6 **Citadel** - prayer warrior and intercessor.

Growth in prayer produces a beautiful and powerful and high level ministry. Not only are other people blessed from our prayers but we are also blessed, in various and manifold ways, from spending so much time in God's Presence.

For a long time, I thought that the sixth vision was the last one. However recently a new vision has come. There is another level after that of intercession and it is the lofty level of being a worshiper.

The **Seventh Vision** was of showering mists, reflecting mirrors, a glowing and radiant Light where one goes upward and then finds themselves on their knees, and three new sweaters woven with blue, purple, and scarlet. The showering mists reminded me of the metal sea before the temple of God. This is where the priests washed themselves before entering the holy place.

II Chronicles 4:2-6 Also he made the cast metal sea, ten cubits from brim to brim, circular in form, and its height was five cubits and its circumference was thirty cubits. [3] Now figures like oxen were under it and all around it, ten cubits, entirely encircling the sea. The oxen were in two rows, cast in one piece. [4] It stood on twelve oxen, three facing north, three facing west, three facing south and three facing east; and the sea was set on top of them, and all their hind-quarters turned inwards. [5] And it was a handbreadth thick, and its brim was made like the brim of a cup, like a lily blossom; it could hold 3,000 baths. [6] He also made ten basins in which to wash, and he set five on the right side and five on the left side, to rinse things for the burnt offering; but the sea was for the priests to wash in.

Perhaps the mirrors are to reflect the Lord's image in us and yea even the fruits of His Spirit. Of course, the glowing and radiant Light that draws us upward and onto our knees is the Lord Himself.

The sweaters were woven with the same colors used in the curtains and veil of the temple (Exodus, Chapter 26). The sweaters appear to be like the covering of a mantle.

The word "worshiper" was given along with this vision. A worshiper is like a priest or a Levite. They sing to the Lord, praise Him, minister to Him, teach His words to the people, and belong to the Lord. They offer the peoples' sacrifices to God so that the people might be forgiven and then they bless the people with God's blessings.

This Last Vision is still new and not fully worked out in my life, yet. So, I can only guess at the cleansing, healing, oneness, restoration and rewards that it hints at. Truly a worshiper is a mature Christian, a joyous person, one who sees God in everything and knows that problems will turn into blessings. A worshiper is also a refuge for the weak and a speaker of God's Words. This is a life of unbroken communion with the Lord - of constantly asking His help and just as frequently giving thanks for the help received.

A worshiper is a temple of God's Spirit, yea even of God Himself!

Desire therefore, to speak God's Words, letting God do His work through you as Jesus spoke the Father's Words. For Jesus' whole ministry was words. He taught with words, healed with words, calmed the wind and the waves with words, and fed the five thousand with words. Moreover, God even created the universe with words.

Whereupon, I will conclude this chapter by telling you that

real power and authority comes from walking with Christ and speaking and praying His words.

And Christ will come again and all dominion in heaven and on earth has been given to Him.
And may the grace of God be with you all. Amen.

16

VICTORIES, BLESSINGS
AND TEACHINGS FROM CANCER

I thought this book was finished and years have passed, but I feel the need to share with you, dear readers, what God taught me when I had cancer.

First of all, I want to tell you that I felt wonderful going through the outpatient surgery and the sixteen days of radiation. This good feeling came from being close to God. I was prayed up, confessed up, interceded up and praised up. I was also in the Word, especially the Psalms.

After I received the call that I had breast cancer, I asked God why He let His daughter have cancer and then I went and did a puzzle. The next day I read the Bible and a teaching about three men in the Bible came to me. I was taught three things about each of these men.

1 These three men all went through hard times and it was "not" because of sin in their lives.
2 God was with them in their hard times - teaching, training and yes, even blessing them.

3 After this testing (training) time came to an end, they were rewarded.

DAVID

The first man was David. His hard time was when King Saul and his armies tried to kill him. David hadn't done anything wrong and his life was in danger and he was afraid. A couple of times David was in a position to take Saul's life but he learned to leave vengeance up to the Lord.

When this difficult time came to an end God rewarded David by making him a great king in Israel. The years of testing and training with God made him a wise ruler and not a selfish dictator.

JOSEPH

The second man was Joseph. His hard time was when his brothers sold him into slavery. Some of his brothers even wanted to kill him. God was with him in slavery and blessed his work and he was put in charge of all the other slaves. After a while the owner's wife tried to seduce Joseph and then falsely accused him. He ended up in Pharaoh's prison where God again lifted him up to be in charge of the other prisoners.

Eventually, Joseph learned to hear God's still small voice and he interpreted the dreams of Pharaoh's baker and wine-cup bearer. A couple years passed before Joseph was called to interpret Pharaoh's dreams.

Joseph's reward was to be raised up second to Pharaoh in the land. He had power and wealth and he handled it wisely because of his training.

When Joseph was young he had a dream that his parents and his brothers bowed down to him. Well, after a number of years had gone by and during the seven-year famine, all of Egypt bowed down to Joseph as he fed them. His dream took a while to be answered and then it was answered in a much bigger way.

JOB

The third man was Job. He was a Godly man who lost his children, wealth from his sheep and other animals, and his health. He wanted to talk to God face to face and find out why all this bad stuff happened to him.

His friends came to comfort him and took one look at him and decided he must have some secret sin in his life. Thus, his so-called comforters became his accusers. During this time, Job said, "My redeemer lives." At the end of the book, Job did get to talk with the Lord and found out how very big his God was. God was displeased with Job's comforters and He had Job intercede for them. After that Job was Rewarded Double.

MY REWARD

After the radiation was over (for a two to three-month period) all of my prayers were answered and right away. A couple prayers were big ones such as new jobs for relatives. I remember my brother telling me of an answer to prayer that I had just prayed for the day before. I was in awe of God and certainly didn't deserve all these blessings.

*   *   *

Our wonderful Lord added one more thing to this time of teaching. He said:

Now I want you to pray grown-up prayers —
Now I want you to say adult prayers —
I Gave You My Name – Now Use It!

Jesus' name is over everything in heaven and earth.

You can pray cancer out of someone's body in Jesus' Name and they can go into remission. This prayer can even be done at a distance. I always follow up these "authority prayers" by praying Jesus' life, health, strength and wholeness back into them.

When there is strong discord between relatives, friends or co-workers and counseling and Scripture doesn't seem to work – then it's time for spiritual warfare and I pray everything out of that person that is not from God, **In JESUS' Name**, and follow up with praying Jesus and His blessings, His love, His peace, and His truth back into them.

How blessed it is to always be able to grow more like Jesus and to hear His still small voice – what an awesome feeling that is!

17

TELL THE LORD

Oh, my beloved child, I am calling you closer so that you can enter into my rest. Come let us walk in the garden together and see the beauty of the flowers. I shall embrace thee and care for thee and give thee of My perfection - yea even of My cleanness, goodness, healthiness and life.

Precious child, I have given you steps to grow in Me. I would that ye grow and mature in wisdom and might. Yes, I would have ye stand strong in the midst of distress, and look to Me and trust Me. I would have ye become a sanctuary (priest, worshiper), yea, even a pillar that others might look to you and become strengthened.

Return to Me and return to My word that I might restore blessings to you. For, how can I stand you all downcast and ill? Return to My Love so that I can return to you and heal you. Let Me abide in you that you may be built up as My priest and become a sanctuary where others might come and find shelter in a weary land. You need speak only a few words - when they are My Words - to bless others and give love, peace, joy, strength, wisdom, encouragement, understanding, counsel, mercy, power and whatever is needed.

Try Me and see that I AM good. Read My Words before you go to sleep and see that you sleep more soundly and arise more refreshed. Ask My help with whatever you do. I give you free will and how can I help you if you do not ask? Nothing is too big or too small to tell Me about.

Behold your Lord - the One who is trustworthy - the One who loves you! Behold also the One who gives new life - abundant life - and good, joyful, blessed and healthy life.

Believe those who have followed My way and have found happiness. Believe also in Me. How else can you be Light and Salt? I AM the Way, the Truth, and the Life.

Why carry those burdens, fears, insecurities, and unrest around any longer? Come to Me, even you who are leaders, come closer. Behold Me and become like Me. Man may fail you but I never will.

Do not doubt Me when we both work together to mature you so that you can receive more blessings. I AM always here for you - My love readily available. My understanding, My wisdom and My help are eager to be given. Just ask. Share yourself with Me so that I may share Myself with you. I AM the perfect parent, perfect friend, perfect teacher, perfect comforter and perfect companion. Yes, I AM all in all!

Remember My child how My way is not your way. You see another affliction but I see My anointing resting heavily upon you, you're being a great blessing to others, and the victories that are coming.

When Paul called himself a prisoner of Christ, he was not just being sweet. No, this innocent man was actually in prison. And it was during these prison times when he was most used and the greatest blessing. Generation after generation of peoples are blessed by the books of the Bible that he wrote during these times. See your unwanted situations as prison times. Respond the way Paul did with praise so that I can break the chains and save many lives (Acts 16). And notice Paul's fantastic opportunities to witness before Felix and Festus as he gave thanks again and again in those unwanted situations. Oh, my child, learn the secret of seeing Me in problems and begin to trust that I will bring victory out of them. Accept My Presence and My inner peace and be a vessel for My healing power like Paul was on the Isle of Malta (Acts 28). Put aside your own reasoning and striving and struggling and the resentments they bring and take My hand and together we shall walk on in gentleness and greatness.

And now My child, it is a time of being reborn again. Like Abraham before him, Jacob also returned to his beginning walk with Me. He was fearful of the numerous Canaanites and so he journeyed closer to Me, the God who answered him in the day of his distress and was with him wherever he traveled (Genesis 35).

- As you draw closer to your first Love (Revelation 2:4),
- I shall again fill you with greater amounts of restoration, and revelation, and blessings and fulfill the plans that I have for your life (Jeremiah 29:11- 12).
- Fill your homes with beautiful music and your minds with My Words; look to Me, and talk to Me and nothing shall be impossible for us. (Matthew 17:20)

Yes, walk in the Light and draw upon My Life and My health and pray My Healing Scriptures into your mind, daily. Verily, you shall receive of this magnificent Love that not only died for you but also lives for you.

And ye shall surely mature in Me and be like the ending chapters in the Book of Psalms - a vessel increasingly filled with praise and victory and triumph. Yea, even filled with Me and One with My Words and My Glory! What a beautiful and righteous and magnetic vessel you will be. And all people will long to spend time with you.

Come all who are willing. There is much to be revealed from My Word and I long to do it. Habakkuk came to Me and complained of the rich getting richer and the poor becoming poorer and of the greed, oppression, and violence in the land. I told him that I was bringing the Babylonians against my people - so that my people would return to me and I could again bless them - and then I would punish the Babylonians. It is not My wish to use hard times to return My people to Me, but their rebellion and their Forgetting Me that brings such about.

Verily, I tell you that the righteous shall live by their faith.

After Habakkuk comes the book of Zephaniah. His name means God will hide His worshiper in times of danger. Yes, I am fully able to protect the humble worshiper, though danger be on the right side and on the left side, it will not touch him.

Haggai and Malachi follow next in the Bible, and they say to awaken and rebuild the temple so that the blessings might be restored. The temple is now you, My beloved child. You will become My priests and be built up as you spend time in My Word and talk with Me. Tell Me everything and I will become real to you and you will grow into a sanctuary. This is relationship! This is abiding! This is being Light and Salt! This is power when you take My Presence and My Words wherever you go. Praise the Lord! Together we can overcome troops and jump over a wall.

My Psalms of Ascents (Psalms 120-134) reveal how a people called to be My priests turn to the Lord in problems, trust and stand strong in the Lord, work together in peace and unity, and become intercessors in the night watches

My love is freely and continually given. Ye need not earn it. Yea, ye cannot earn it. Does anyone love you enough to die for you like I did on the cross? I take no delight in your struggling on your own though darkness and sickness. I long to help you and heal you. Come to Me and tell Me all that you need help with, moment by moment. Ask Me - Praise Me. Know ye not that I AM Creator of the world.

My precious child, I'll let you in on a little secret. It is impossible for the vast fears and worries and stresses of life to remain in you when you are filled with Me. Truly they cannot occupy the same space that I occupy. Moreover, in returning to Me is your peace and your strength. So, keep on returning, and I will keep on blessing you and rewarding you. Never worry about a ministry, My child. Just go on caring for your family and relatives and jobs. For anywhere and everywhere that you are – if you are filled with Me - you will be in My will. So, enter My gates with thanksgiving and My courts with praise and I, and only I, will set up future ministries and nothing shall hinder Me. Receive now of My strength and My health and My joy.

My words will reveal the end times to you. Ezekiel, Daniel, Revelation, Matthew 24, Thessalonians and many places throughout My Word tell of the great tribulation and restoration to come.

All who call upon My Name shall be saved (Acts 2:21). I desire that you call upon My Name. I have loved you since I saw you formed in the womb. I AM the Savior! I CAN forgive you when you cannot forgive yourself.

Surely you know in My Word of the woman caught in adultery and of the woman at the well (who after five husbands was now living with another man). I, the Lord would not let others condemn them, nor would I condemn them. I received them just as they were, loved them, gave them of My life, and sent them out to go and sin no more. Moreover, as My priests, you will need to know this power of forgiveness and extend it to My many people.

For verily I, the Lord, tell you that there is a quiet pouring out of My Spirit going on today and I am quietly and secretly raising up a people called to be My priests. Truly, like the Levites of old, my priests will belong to Me, minister to Me, offer up the problems and sins of others, speak my Words, grow strong in prayer, teach the people about Me, and become worshipers.

And they will be wondrously amazed at the many answered prayers and the spectacular teachings from My Word that come without any effort on their parts. To whoever has, more will be given and come all who are thirsty. Just seek Me and you will enter this quiet outpouring of the Holy Spirit while the worldly goes unaware about their business.

Truly, there is an empty place inside everyone that can only be filled with My deep and abiding Love. Talk to Me and know Me and let My grace abound to you. And surely goodness and mercy shall follow you all the days of your life, and you will dwell in the house of the Lord forever! And may you go about doing good as Jesus did, and receive a double portion and be called the Blessed of the Lord! Amen!

BENEDICTION

May God fill your heart with His love. May He open your eyes to see as He sees. And may He give you His Words to speak, so that you are blessed and then become a blessing to others.

REFERENCES

The PRACTICE of the PRESENCE of GOD, by Brother Lawrence.
Published by Fleming H. Revell Co.

HINDS FEET on HIGH PLACES, by Hannah Hurnard.
Tyndale House publishers Inc.

PRISON to PRAISE, by Merlyn Carothers. Bridge – Logos publishers.

Judy is a rural housewife from Wisconsin. She came from a good but a non-Christian family. After the birth of her children and then moving away from her family, she turned to the Lord for help in becoming a better wife, mother and human being.

Learning the bible and growing in prayer brought her love, peace, joy and blessings. Now her heart is filled with thanksgiving and she feels led to walk in love and grow stronger in prayer.

Made in the USA
Lexington, KY
07 July 2017